GOSPEL OF LIFE

Theology in the Fourth Gospel

G. R. BEASLEY-MURRAY

HENDRICKSON
PUBLISHERS
PEABODY, MASSACHUSETTS 01961-3473

Copyright © 1991 by Hendrickson Publishers, Inc.
P. O. Box 3473
Peabody, Massachusetts, 01961–3473
All rights reserved
Printed in the United States of America

ISBN 0–943575–76–1

Library of Congress Cataloging-in-Publication Data

Beasley-Murray, George Raymond, 1916–
    Gospel of life: theology in the fourth Gospel / G. R.
Beasley-Murray
        p.   cm. — (The 1990 Payton lectures)
    Includes bibliographical references and index.
    ISBN 0–943575–76–1 (pbk.)
    1. Bible.   N.T. John—Theology.   I. Title   II. Series:
Payton lectures: 1990.
BS2615.2.B384   1991
226.5′06—dc20   91-34426
                                                                                   CIP

TABLE OF CONTENTS

Preface

THIS BOOK REPRESENTS THE 1990 Payton Lectures, in a slightly expanded form, delivered at the Fuller Theological Seminary, Pasadena, California, April 10–12, 1990.

The invitation to give these lectures was extended by Dr. Robert Meye, then Dean of the School of Theology in the Fuller Theological Seminary. To him and to Dr. David Hubbard, the president of the seminary, and to their colleagues in the School of Theology, I owe a debt of gratitude for the welcome accorded to me and my wife. Fuller Seminary is a great institution; it performs a valuable task in equipping men and women for a great variety of Christian ministries, within and without the U.S.A. It was a privilege for me to serve the school in a modest way.

All the themes discussed in this work could have, and have had, monographs devoted to them. No attempt has been made to be exhaustive in the treatment of the subjects here offered; rather, an approach has been made to an understanding and solution of the problems entailed in them. For fuller exegetical treatment of the relevant passages in the Fourth Gospel the interested reader is referred to the writer's commentary on the Gospel of John in the Word Biblical Commentary, volume 36, published by Word Books, Publisher, Dallas, Texas.

INTRODUCTION

C HRISTIAN THEOLOGY IS THE STORY of Jesus interpreted by the aid of the Spirit of God. "Gospel," said J. Becker in apparent agreement, ". . . is exposition of the saving action of God in Christ."[1] That is the presupposition of the primitive "kerygma"— the good news of Jesus Messiah and Lord which lies behind the written Gospels—and of the Gospels themselves which embody it, and it is the foundation of the rest of the writings of the New Testament.

Naturally the story of Jesus did not arise as though it were an isolated episode of ancient Middle Eastern history. It is portrayed as the climax of God's dealings with a nation chosen by God to accomplish his good purpose for all nations. That, too, is a story, a history of the acts of God for the salvation and judgment of a people, interpreted as significant for the salvation and judgment of all humanity.

This understanding of the Bible was fundamental for those who wrote it and preserved it. The Hebrew Bible was divided by the Jews into three parts, the Law, the Prophets, and the Writings, and this division is assumed in the New Testament (cf. Luke 24:44). The central feature of the first section is the story of God's leading a family, whose descendants he "redeemed" from slavery to become his covenant people and to receive his law. "The Prophets" include the historical works that narrate the ongoing history of this elect people and books containing oracles of God, given through their prophets during their long history. "The Writings" presuppose those same acts of God, which inspired their praise and prayers and their understanding of the divine revelation. It is evident, accordingly, that for the Jew the revelation of God was indissolubly bound up with the history of his people. It was revelation in history interpreted through prophetic souls. The Gospels relate the climax of this historical revelation in the acts and words of God in and through Jesus, by which the promised saving sovereignty (= kingdom) of god was initiated and the revelation fulfilled. The remaining works of the New Testament unfold and expound that revelation.

No individual in the primitive church understood this more clearly than the Fourth Evangelist. That "Christian theology is the story of Jesus interpreted" is peculiarly true of his Gospel. It is unashamedly a theological history, written to lay bare the revelation embodied in the word and work of Jesus, Son of Man–Son of God, Messiah, and Word of God. In this respect it consummates the theology set forth in the synoptic tradition, though admittedly with the aid of elements preserved in its own unique tradition (cf. the exposition of the Word of God in the Prologue). This has been recognized by interpreters of the Gospel through the ages. It is assumed in the well-known statement of Clement of Alexandria, wherein he contrasted the earlier Gospels with that of John: the former set forth the "bodily facts" about Jesus, whereas the latter is a "spiritual gospel."[2] Not that this contrast should be overdrawn. B. F. Westcott, for example, was well aware that to view the synoptic Gospels as historical and the Fourth Gospel as doctrinal is simplistic, since all the evangelists wrote in the conviction that Christian doctrine is embedded in the history of Jesus. He affirmed:

> The synoptic narratives are implicit dogmas, no less truly than St. John's dogmas are concrete facts. The real difference is that the earliest Gospel contained the fundamental facts and words which experience afterwards interpreted, while the latest Gospel reviews the facts in the light of their interpretation.[3]

Whether the Fourth Evangelist knew and used the first three Gospels is a long contested issue, but there can be no doubt that he knew and utilized at least the traditions underlying those Gospels. E. M. Sidebottom begged no questions when he spoke of the Fourth Gospel as a complement to the others, "not in the sense that it interprets them, but that it shows us how to interpret them."[4]

This interpretative function of the Fourth Gospel has led a long line of critics to reject its testimony root and branch. It is comprehensible, and indeed instructive, that the roots of this rejection go back to the English Deists[5] and that it was popularized by David Strauss.[6] The chief elements of offense are the divergence between the synoptists and John in their records of the history of Jesus, but above all in their representation of his teaching, i.e., in the theology of the Gospels. This was unambiguously stated by K. Lake:

> Since the Johannine narrative is so different from (the synoptics) it must be largely, if not entirely, fictitious and written by a Hellenistic Christian in order to support the sacramental theology which finds a centre in the divine Jesus.[7]

The change of mood in Johannine studies during the latter half of the twentieth century is strikingly illustrated by an utterance of C. H. Dodd, opening his summary and conclusion to the most exhaustive and careful examination ever given to the comparison of the history of Jesus in the synoptics and in the Fourth Gospel. The statement is worded with Dodd's characteristic caution:

> The above argument has led to the conclusion that behind the Fourth Gospel lies an ancient tradition independent of the other gospels, and meriting serious consideration as a contribution to our knowledge of the historical facts concerning Jesus Christ.[8]

In reality the church through the ages has accounted for the unique representation of Jesus in the Gospel of John in terms of the illumination of the evangelist's mind by the Holy Spirit, the "other Paraclete" promised by the Lord to follow on his own ministry (see John 14:16–17, 25–26, etc.). That still holds good of the great majority of critical scholars, but they add to this postulate of faith supporting features drawn from their own expertise. J. A. T. Robinson, for example, stresses the symbolic significance of every detail of this Gospel, "resonant with overtones for those with ears to hear them," and he urges: "The theology is drawing out the history rather than creating it or even moulding it."[9] In his view there are three ways of seeing Christ in the Fourth Gospel: (1) On the outside, as eyes see on the level of the flesh; this is the level of the Jews who saw without believing (6:36), even without really seeing (6:26). (2) From the outside in, which is the first approach of everyone who believes through seeing. (3) From the inside out, i.e., of those who see from within, in the Spirit, for whom flesh is shot through with glory and truth.[10] These distinctions were doubtless an application of that drawn by the historian R. G. Collingwood between "the outside" and "the inside" of the same event, between what can be described externally and that which can be described in terms of thought.[11] Robinson cites at length T. E. Pollard's use of Collingwood's differentiation:

> Applying this distinction I would say that the Synoptists are more concerned with the "outside" of the events they record, even though they record them because they believe that they have a theological or soteriological significance. John, on the other hand, is concerned with the "inside" of the events... The Synoptists see Jesus and his words and actions from the outside through the eyes of the disciples; John "enters sympathetically into the mind" of Jesus, or "puts himself into the shoes" of Jesus. . . .

This leads Pollard to assert:

> On Collingwood's definition of the real task of the historian, it could well be argued that John is a better historian that the Synoptists. John portrays Jesus as the one who at every point is conscious of his Messianic function as Son of God, whose every action, thought and word are governed by this consciousness. There is no need to interpret this portrait as an invention of John or a falsification of what Jesus really was. Rather it is an attempt to portray Jesus as he was, in his earthly life, in and for himself. It is not that this Jesus of St. John is any less human than the Jesus of the Synoptics; it is rather that John penetrates with deeper insight into the inner springs of the personality of Jesus. Nor was John's portrait a more highly developed theological interpretation; rather because of his deeper insight he makes explicit what is implicit, and, for the most part, veiled in the synoptics.[12]

Experience shows that it is they who "enter sympathetically into the mind of Jesus" with the evangelist's aid who understand his Gospel best and bring to light its hidden profundities. Curiously, this very sentiment was uttered by the earliest commentator on the Gospel of John in the orthodox church, namely Origen, who affirmed that nobody could perceive the meaning of the Fourth Gospel who had not leaned on Jesus' breast and taken from Jesus Mary as his own mother.[13] That implies the necessity for the discerning reader to enter into the same kind of profound fellowship that the Beloved Disciple experienced with the Son of God, the evangelist had predicated

upontheSon'srelationshipwiththeFather(with13:23cf.1:18).
It is often thought that the Gospel, along with other Johannine writings, emanated from "the School of John." It is
good to recognize that believers may enroll in that School
today! For our encouragement it may be said that the "School"
continues to flourish. Rarely have so many outstanding works
on the Fourth Gospel emanated from its ranks as in our time.
One of the most notable examples of tarrying in the company
of the Beloved Disciple happens to be of one who spent almost
all his life pondering and familiarizing himself with the Gospel
in the latter half of the nineteenth century, B. F. Westcott, whose
great commentary did not see the light of day till the present
century, after his death, but the influence of which still endures.
A successor in like arduous labors to gain an understanding of
the Gospel was Sir Edwyn Hoskyns, whose wrestling with the
text produced the most genuinely theological exposition of the
Gospel that has appeared, even though the final revision of his
exegesis did not reach beyond chapter 6. The reading of that
work I found to be a profound spiritual experience. Hoskyns
recognized that there was a workshop in which the Fourth Gospel was fashioned, filled with particular ideas and experiences
and even other Christian literature, but that in the writing of
his Gospel the evangelist covered up his tracks, for "his theme
is not his own workshop by the workshop of God!"[14] In that
hallowed place Hoskyns conceived the evangelist to have seen
his vision of Christ:

> Faced by the life and death of Jesus, in its general of in its particular
> details, the Fourth Evangelist knows that he is confronted by what
> is infinite and eternal. He finds himself standing as a point where
> all things become well nigh transparent, where he is able to see
> what no eye hath seen. For in the flesh of Jesus he sees, not only
> his eternal sonship, but also the eternal sonship of his disciples;
> not only the eternal sonship of his disciples, but the light which
> lighteth every man. And we dare not say that what he has seen is
> illusion, or merely an interpretation. For what he has seen does
> make sense of the fragments recorded in the synoptic gospels.[15]

That expresses the present writer's convictions concerning the
testimony of the Fourth Gospel to Jesus. These convictions are
the fount from which the reflections on the theology of the
Gospel expressed in this book rise.

NOTES TO INTRODUCTION

1. J. Becker, *Das Evangelium des Johannes*, Ökumenischer Taschenbuch-Kommentar zum Neuen Testament 4/1, Gütersloh, 1979, 38.

2. Reported by Eusebius in his *History of the Church* 3.31,3.

3. *The Gospel According to John*, vol. 1, lxxxiv–lxxxv, London, 1908.

4. *The Christ of the Fourth Gospel*, London, 1961, 187.

5. In his work *The Dissonance of the Four Generally Received Evangelists*, published in 1792, E. Evanson emphasized the contrasts between the Fourth Gospel and the book of Revelation; he maintained that the former was written by a Platonic philosopher of the second century.

6. Strauss' epoch-making work, *Das Leben Jesu*, Berlin, 1835–36, appeared in English in 1846 as *The Life of Jesus Critically Examined*, translated from the 4th edition by George Eliot (without mention of her name!). Strauss considered that the Fourth Gospel had no value as a historical source, insofar as it advanced the mythical view of Jesus in the synoptic Gospels and was controlled by theological and apologetic motives. A perceptive summary of Strauss' thought concerning the Fourth Gospel is given by A. Schweitzer in his *Quest of the Historical Jesus*, London, 1910 (2d ed., 1911) 85–88.

7. *An Introduction to the New Testament*, London, 1938, 51.

8. *Historical Tradition in the Fourth Gospel*, Cambridge, 1963, 423.

9. *The Priority of John*, London, 1985, 297.

10. Ibid., 345–46.

11. Collingwood, *The Idea of History*, Oxford, 1959, 174.

12. "St. John's Contribution to the Picture of the Historical Jesus," an inaugural lecture at Knox Theological Hall, Dunedin N.Z. 1964, published in *Forum*, 16.6 (a journal for ministers of the Presbyterian Church of N.Z.), cited by Robinson, *Priority*, 362–63.

13. *In Ioannem* 1.6.

14. *The Fourth Gospel*, ed. F. N. Davey, London, 2d ed., 1947, 18.

15. Ibid., 130.

CHAPTER 1

THE GOSPEL OF LIFE

THE WRITER TO THE HEBREWS introduced a quotation from the Old Testament with the words, "Someone somewhere solemnly said" (Heb. 2:6). Dr. Percy Evans, a revered lecturer in my student days, was encouraged and comforted by those words; he never did find it easy to remember Scripture references! I, too, have reason to share his comfort. Years ago I read somewhere a statement which considerably impressed me; I have sought in vain in my books to find its author. This scholar affirmed, "The term salvation is not in the vocabulary of Jesus." I shall hold back a moment to tell you the word which, in his estimate, Jesus used instead, and request that that statement be allowed to sink in. When we reflect on the frequency with which modern preachers of the gospel take that word on their lips, it is remarkable if in fact Jesus never used it. In reality it is not quite correct that Jesus *never* used the term. Certainly it does not occur at all in the Gospels of Matthew and Mark. It is found once in a saying of Jesus in Luke, and once in John. In the conversation with the Samaritan woman at the well Jesus said to her, "Salvation is of the Jews" (John 4:22), which is not exactly an epitome of the gospel. But Luke records one occasion when Jesus employed the term in a manner akin to our use of it. Having declared to Zacchaeus his desire to enter his house, and having heard the intention of Zacchaeus to restore what he had wrongfully taken from the people, Jesus said to his shocked critics, "Today salvation has come to this house, since he also is a son of Abraham"

(Luke 19:9). And that is the sum total of Jesus' employment of the word salvation.

What word, then, did Jesus use to convey the concept of salvation when he made known the gospel to his contemporaries? My anonymous instructor replied: "Life." Now it would be possible to contest that answer, for we all know that in the first three Gospels the expression most frequently on the lips of Jesus is "the kingdom of God." It is, however, increasingly acknowledged that "kingdom of God" denotes not a territory over which God rules, or a people over whom he rules, but the putting forth of the almighty power of God as sovereign Lord of the universe to save. "Kingdom of God" is a dynamic expression, and for that reason it is often replaced by the phrase "the sovereignty of God," understood as God acting in fulfillment of his promise to bring salvation to his people. That is clear, but what is the effect or result of people opening their lives to that saving sovereignty of God? In the teaching of Jesus, as in Jewish writings contemporary with the New Testament, the supreme blessing of the kingdom of God is "life." For that reason it is often spoken of as "eternal life," since it is life in the eternal kingdom, or as the Jews often put it, the life of the age to come. It is of no small significance that the term "life," or "eternal life," occurs many more times in the Fourth Gospel than in any of the first three Gospels. Indeed, it is not too much to say that the key term of Jesus for salvation appropriated is the key term of the Gospel of John. The evangelist himself stated that the reason for his writing his Gospel was, "that you may believe that Jesus is the Christ, the Son of God, and that through believing you may have life in his name" (John 20:31).

While the first three Gospels use the word "life" less frequently than the Fourth Gospel, their authors knew perfectly well what it meant. Mark records some strong words of Jesus about taking radical action to ensure that one gains the life that God alone can bestow. "If your hand causes your downfall, cut it off; it is better for you to enter into *life* maimed than to keep both hands and go to hell, to the unquenchable fire" (Mark 9:43). The same is said about the offending foot or eye; better to "enter life" crippled or one-eyed than to have both feet and both eyes and be sent off to Gehenna (Mark 9:43–48). "To enter life" and to go to Gehenna are contrasted destinies. To enter life means to participate in the life of the kingdom of God.

A further instructive example of the associations of the term "life" in the synoptic record is seen in the Markan account of the Rich Young Ruler's encounter with Jesus (Mark 10:17–31). The young man runs to Jesus and asks him what he must do to "inherit" eternal life. Jesus tells him to keep the commands. He declares that he always has, so Jesus points to the one thing he lacks: he should give away his possessions to the poor and so gain "treasure in heaven." Jesus then invites him to join his company of disciples. This he is unwilling to do, and he turns away and departs. Whereupon Jesus observes how difficult it is for those with wealth to enter the kingdom of God. When the disciples express amazement at such an idea, on the assumption that the wealthy have their riches as a favor from God, Jesus applies the observation generally: "My boys, how difficult it is for anyone to enter the kingdom of God!" With yet greater astonishment they ask, "Who then can be saved?" And Jesus replies, "Nobody. Only God can do that for people!" On their indignation reaching explosion point Jesus assures them that all who have sacrificed for his sake and the gospel's will be rewarded by God in this time, and in the age to come they will have "eternal life." The point of interest is the synonyms that occur in this narrative: "inherit eternal life," "treasure in heaven" (i.e., with God), "enter the kingdom of God," "be saved," "eternal life in the age to come." All represent a gift which God alone can give, and their employment as synonymous expressions throws light on the meaning of each. Observe, however, that it does not follow that "kingdom of God" and "life" (or "life eternal") are equivalents. "Kingdom of God" is the sovereign action of God for the salvation of humankind, an activity which is destined to embrace the universe; "life" or "life eternal" is blessed existence under that saving sovereignty, with all the consequences that ensue from that. In the Mark 10 passage it is entry into the kingdom of God that is paralleled with eternal life.

Now there is a major difference between the concept of "life" in the Fourth Gospel and that in the Old Testament, early Jewish literature, and the synoptic Gospels: in all these latter writings "life" or "eternal life" is a future hope, since it is life in the kingdom of God that is to come; in the Fourth Gospel, however, it is characteristically the gift of God given in the present time. Of the many examples that can be adduced from the Gospel to illustrate the point, the clearest and most startling one is John 5:24: "Amen, amen I say to you, he who hears my word and believes on him who sent me has eternal life; he does not come into condemnation but has crossed over from death to life" (see further 3:36; 4:14; 6:47, 53; 17:3).

When the question is asked how this difference is to be explained, students of the Fourth Gospel agree that it is due above all to the evangelist's reflection on the significance of Jesus, that is to say on his Christology. He has grasped and carried to the limit the profound truth, expressed elsewhere in the New Testament, that eschatology is Christology.

This appears already in the opening paragraph of the Gospel. Of the Logos it is stated:

Everything came into existence through him,
and apart from him not a thing came into being.
What has come into existence had its life in him,
and the life was the light of men (vv. 3–4).

Here the Logos is asserted to be the mediator in creation, alike in its beginning and in its continuance. Doubtless it is humankind that is in view in the second sentence. The Logos-Son is the life and the light of humanity, in creation and in new creation. While the gospel emphasizes the latter aspect, the new creative work of the Logos-Christ presupposes his original creative action and his role in the achievement of its goal. This inclusive function of the Son comes to expression in 5:26, "Just as the Father has life in himself, so also he has granted the Son to have life in himself."

That "gift" of the Father to the Son must be assumed to be prior to creation, but the Gospel is concerned to show how the life of the new creation has become possible for the world through the Son of God. It is none other than the life of God, mediated through the Son. Revealed in his incarnate life, it became available for all humanity through his death and resurrection. That is epitomized in the famous John 3:16, and in the sentences that both follow and precede it: "As Moses lifted up the snake in the desert, so the Son of Man must be lifted up, in order that everyone who believes may have *in him* eternal life." The life eternal is participation in the life of God in Christ by virtue of his sacrifice and exaltation.

While the Gospel majors on the presence of the life that has come to humankind in Christ, there are not lacking references to a future dimension of this life for those who are its recipients.

"Life eternal" inevitably calls to mind the future that flows from the present. It is life in the saving sovereignty of God that has no end. One thinks of the saying of Jesus to the people who searched for him after the miracle of the loaves: "You should work not for food that perishes but for food that lasts for eternal life, which the Son of Man will give to you" (6:27). Yet more clearly capturing this future dimension is 12:25, which recalls a synoptic saying (Mark 8:35 par; Matt. 10:39; Luke 9:24): "Anyone who loves his life loses it, and anyone who hates his life in this world will preserve it for eternal life." In this latter saying one hears an echo of the distinction between "this age" and "the age to come," beloved of apocalyptic and rabbinic thought (see further 4:36; 5:39; 6:40, 54, 68; 10:28). Mussner cites with approval the view of A. Titius that all the "life eternal" passages, even where they have to do with present possession, have through the attribute *aiōnios* (eternal) an eschatological tone.[1]

There are references in the Gospel to a future resurrection, notably 5:28–29, and four passages in chapter 6, where mention is made of resurrection through Christ "in the last day" (vv. 39, 40, 44, 54). This dual concept of resurrection to life now and resurrection to life in the future is paralleled with other future eschatological expectations, such as judgment—in the present (12:31–32) and in the future (12:47); the parousia—in the future (14:3) and anticipated in the present (14:23); and the kingdom of God, with which both future eschatological hope and present eschatological possession are bound. Similarly John 3:3 and 5, and 18:36 can all be related to both present and future experience and hope.

This juxtaposition of present and future eschatologies within the one Gospel has proved too much for some exegetes to accept. Bultmann's views on this theme have greatly influenced succeeding scholars. He considered that the Fourth Evangelist, by his relating eschatological hope to the redemptive action of Christ in the present, "historicized" or "demythologized" eschatology. His comment on John 12:31 is well known:

> The judgment of this world now takes place. The ruler of this world will now be thrown out of the domain over which he formerly held sway. The significance of the hour of decision is thus described in the cosmological terminology of the Gnostic myth. If in the evan-

gelist's mind the myth has lost its mythological context and become historicized, his language on the other hand serves to eliminate the traditional eschatology of primitive Christianity. The turn of the ages results now. . . . Since this "now" the "prince of the world" is judged (16:11); the destiny of man has become definitive, according as each grasps the meaning of this "now," according as he believes or not. *No future in this world's history can bring anything new, and all apocalyptic pictures of the future are empty dreams.*[2]

In Bultmann's estimate the references in the Fourth Gospel to resurrection and judgment "on the last day" are due to modifications of the text by an "ecclesiastical redactor." In the Upper Room discourses the placing of Easter, Pentecost, and the parousia in close proximity is believed to show that they are not three separate events but one: "The one event that is meant by all these is not an external occurrence, but an inner one, the victory which Jesus wins when faith arises in man by the overcoming of the offense that Jesus is to him."[3]

While Bultmann's attribution to an ecclesiastical redactor of references to future eschatology in John has been rejected by most scholars, the idea that the evangelist radically reinterpreted the primitive Christian eschatology has been widely taken up. Most commonly it is acknowledged that the evangelist himself retained elements of future eschatology, but that he strictly subordinated them to his emphasis on present fulfillment. Schulz considers that John retained them so as to conduct a polemic against them.

Everything that the traditional expectation of judgment and salvation hoped from the end is related to the present of Jesus in a manifestly polemical sense. . . . His eschatological confession of faith is the once for all and unheard of protest against making the present, which is eschatologically qualified through the coming of Jesus, empty and irrelevant.[4]

This I find difficult to receive. The Fourth Gospel has no explicit polemic against any element of future eschatological hope, whether resurrection, parousia, judgment or kingdom of God, but on the contrary, offers affirmation of them all.

Exegetes tend to speak with several voices on this issue. On the one hand, they affirm that the evangelist retains the earlier eschatological traditions, although these are strictly irreconcilable with his emphasis on the present fulfillment in Christ and

have lost their relevance for him. On the other hand, it is acknowledged that while this is so, the evangelist preserves the
eschatological traditions of the primitive church because he
believes that they contain elements that have not been completely fulfilled through the ministry of the incarnate Redeemer.
The difficulty of bringing these two interpretations together
results in an impression of an evangelist who experienced a
certain confusion in his thought about eschatology or who, to
say the least, succeeded in confusing his readers by his "revolutionary" eschatology. I have to confess that I do not receive
that impression from the Gospel itself, and I was not confused
until I read the interpretations of the exegetes. Let us then see
if we can find some firm ground on which to stand and survey
this disputed territory.

First, it is perhaps not superfluous to recall that the Fourth
Evangelist is not writing a dissertation on the theology of the
primitive *church*, but he is seeking, under the guidance of the
Holy Spirit, to represent the teaching of *Jesus*. The evangelist is
not without constraints in his depiction of the life and teaching
of the incarnate Son. The traditions of the teaching of Jesus
would have been of immense importance to him. It is *these*
which he is recounting and interpreting!

In this connection we should not overlook the affinities between the Fourth Gospel and the Synoptics in this area. In the
latter it is unmistakably evident that Jesus proclaimed the kingdom of God as coming in the future. In spite, however, of the
insistence of those scholars who maintain that for Jesus the
kingdom was *solely* a future phenomenon, most exegetes now
acknowledge that he also declared its presence in his ministry.
Indeed, we must go further and recognize that *the fulfillment
of the promise of the awaited kingdom in his ministry is the
supremely important feature of Jesus' teaching.*[5] It is this which
separates him from all Israel's prophets and apocalyptic seers.
The presence of the kingdom of God in the word and deed of
Jesus signifies God's achieving his sovereign, redemptive will in
and through him. That action came to its climax in Jesus' death
and resurrection, as key sayings of Jesus show, above all his
utterances at the Last Supper. It is therefore false to maintain
that the Fourth Evangelist was being "revolutionary" in attrib-
uting to Jesus teaching that the kingdom of God was present in
him. The "revolution" in eschatology was brought about by

Jesus, whose life and ministry were a revelation of the presence of the kingdom of God, both in its joyous transformation of life and in costly sacrifice. Admittedly, whereas that has to be searched for in the Synoptics, it is "writ large" in the Fourth Gospel, and its significance is continually underscored. Therein lies the immense contribution of the Fourth Evangelist. But it is also to be weighed that, as throughout his ministry, at the Last Supper the Lord made it clear that the kingdom that had come into the world in his ministry was the kingdom destined to embrace the world in the gladness of the feast for the nations, to say nothing of other instruction of his on resurrection, judgment, and parousia. If the Fourth Evangelist reproduces elements of this teaching, as he does, it is at least to be reckoned with that he took such teaching seriously and did not regard it as marginal.

In comparing the synoptic and Johannine representations of the eschatological teaching of Jesus, it is important to bear in mind that in the former the fulfillment of the promise of the kingdom in Jesus is no merely immanent development of the historical process, but the intervention of God in history in and through him. The summary of the message of Jesus in Mark 1:15 means that God's eschatological hour has struck, and God is now stepping into history to accomplish his saving sovereignty. The synoptic teaching on the relation of Jesus to the kingdom of God makes it plain that this eschatological action is accomplished through him; God's present eschatological hour coincides with the presence in the world of the mediator of the kingdom of God. The doctrine of the incarnation in the Fourth Gospel makes the decisiveness of this intervention of God into history transparently clear. But does it change the nature of the divine intervention? Or does it unveil the true character of the intervention of God in Christ narrated by the synoptists?

Johannine scholars frequently see here a contrast between the synoptic *horizontal* line of eschatological action and the Johannine *vertical* line, which, in the view of some, eliminates the former. It is urged by such theologians that this vertical dimension of the divine action presupposes that God in Christ has descended from heaven to redeem his children, and with Christ's having accomplished the redemption, the turn of the ages has taken place; in light of this new situation, no further intervention from above is needful. But why not recognize that *the vertical descent has initiated a horizontal line of continuing eschatological action of God in Christ?*

One could put the issue in different terms by asking whether the decisive eschatological action of God in Christ, as set forth in the Fourth Gospel, *excludes* or *demands* further eschatological action in the future. Bultmann had no doubt about this: we recall his comment on John 12:31: "The turn of the ages results now. . . . No future in this world's history can bring anything new, and all apocalyptic pictures of the future are empty dreams." It is of interest to compare this statement with one by G. Bertram relating to the same passage of the gospel: "Exaltation is . . . *the presupposition of his coming again.*"[6] In making this affirmation Bertram was influenced by W. Thüsing's investigation of this theme, which Thüsing regarded as of crucial importance for understanding early Christology.[7] Thüsing pointed out that in the primitive church the expectation of the returning Lord was always the parousia of the *Risen* Lord, and so there was always a holding together in faith of the Risen One and the Coming One. This is surely correct, and it is reflected in various ways in the synoptic traditions. But does it hold true for the Fourth Gospel?

A crucial test passage for determining this is the well-known reference to the coming of Christ in John 14:2–3:

> In my Father's house there are many dwellings; if it were otherwise I would have told you, for I am going to make ready a place for you. And if I go and make a place ready for you I shall come again and take you with me to my home, that you also may be where I am.

Everybody acknowledges that this is parousia language. The question is what the evangelist wanted his readers to understand by it. A number of exegetes affirm that an authoritative exposition of the passage is provided in the sentences that follow. C. H. Dodd lucidly represented these interpreters. He wrote:

> Christ's "coming again" must be understood in the sense that (a) Christ will continue his mighty works in his disciples (14:12); (b) the Paraclete will dwell in them (14:16–17); (c) they will live by virtue of the living Christ (14:19); and (d) they will continue in a perpetual interchange of *agapē* with him (14:21). In this sense he will come to them (14:18); they will see him, though the world will not (14:19); he will manifest himself to them (14:21).[8]

Now this interpretation raises the question of how it relates to the contemporary belief that "every eye will see him." Dodd sees that difficulty reflected in the exclamation of "Lord, whatever has happened that you will manifest thyself to us and not to the world?" (14:22). "The answer shows that the true parousia is to be found in the interchange of divine agape, made possible through Christ's death and resurrection (14:23)."[9]

At first sight this appears to be a very plausible interpretation of the passage; but it proceeds on the assumption that the parousia can be identified with the resurrection of Jesus, the coming of the Holy Spirit, and the fellowship of Jesus with his disciples. I submit that that assumption entails a confusion of eschatological realities not to be attributed to the evangelist. The discourse of John 14 is a highly compressed presentation of teaching contained in successive paragraphs which require illumination from other passages in the Gospel. For example, in 16:7 Jesus says, "If I do not go away the Paraclete will not come to you; but if I go away I will send him to you." There is no question here of identifying the parousia of Jesus with the coming of the Holy Spirit; on the contrary, the departure of Jesus is the condition of the Spirit's coming. Why must Jesus "go away" in order for the Spirit to "come"? His departure is to take place through his "lifting up" on the cross and to the throne of God, which accomplishes the climax of the coming of God's saving sovereignty for the world; *then* it is that the Spirit of the kingdom of God may commence his ministry of bearing witness to Jesus and bringing about the renewal of humankind (see 7:39; 12:23, 31–32; 13:31–32; 20:22). This is distinct Johannine teaching and should not be changed in the interest of an eschatological theory.

Without doubt John uses the concept of Jesus' "coming" in a complex way. The statement of 14:18, "I will not leave you desolate, I will come to you," manifestly relates to Jesus' dissipating the grief of his disciples by appearing to them in the Easter resurrection, as the expansion of the saying in 16:16–24 shows. The promise is made in 14:21 that this Easter experience will be shared by subsequent believers as they open their lives to Christ in the gospel (14:21), and in 14:23 the post–Easter manifestation of Jesus is presented in terms of a pre-parousia experience of fellowship with the Father and the Son. The latter should no more be viewed as cancelling out the parousia than the sharing in the original disciples' experience of Easter abolishes the reality of the Easter appearances of Jesus. The privileged fellowship of the believer with the Father and the Son is a *foretaste* of the consummate reality of which 14:3 speaks, not an identification with it. The assurance, "I shall come again and take you with me to my home, that you also may be where I am," is a simple, unapocalyptic representation of the coming of the Lord for the perfection of life in the kingdom of God. There is no reductionism in the dialogue that follows the statement, only utterances which indicate the horizontal continuum of the vertical dimension of God's eschatological action in the redemptive work of his incarnate Son.

The essential rightness of this understanding of the eschatological teaching of the Fourth Evangelist finds confirmation in the area with which we began, namely, in his representation of life (eternal). Allow me to offer a series of summary assertions.

(1) The first mention of life in this Gospel is 1:4. "In him was life" affirms primarily the relation of the Logos-Son to creation. It is an assertion of the horizontal relation of the Logos to humanity. (Observe: there is no question of a descent and ascent of the Logos to and from the world in the prologue; on the contrary, the prologue affirms an unbroken activity of the Logos in relation to humankind from creation on.)

(2) The vertical dimension of eschatological action in the incarnation was to bring the life of heaven to the world, i.e., the life of the saving sovereignty of God that restores, renews, and fulfills the life given to humanity in creation. As John 3:3 intimates, it is the life of the new creation.

(3) The possibility of humankind's receiving this life of the saving sovereignty, new creation, or kingdom of God was accomplished in the death and resurrection of Christ, for which purpose he was sent into the world. So we learn in 3:14–15 and the kerygmatic exposition of life and judgment in 3:16–21.

(4) Whoever hears the good news of life through the Son and believes on him has the verdict of acquittal passed on him or her. That person has made the transition from the realm of death to the kingdom of life and consequently "has" the life. This assertion in 5:24 is followed by a statement that defines the "life" in terms of resurrection: the "dead" hear the voice of the Son of God and come to life, for "Just as the Father has life in himself, so also he has granted the Son to have life in himself" (5:26). This metaphorical use of resurrection to life explicitly shows that the life bestowed by the Christ is existence

under the saving sovereignty of God; it is life made possible by the death and resurrection of the incarnate Redeemer.

(5) This teaching is presented in similar terms in 11:25, but in a manner that articulates its real meaning. Martha confidently expresses the Jewish faith in a future resurrection: "I know that he (my brother) will rise in the last day." Jesus replies to her, "I am the resurrection and the life." That corresponds with the statement in 5:26: "He (the Father) has given to the Son to have life in himself." He is the mediator of life in this world and life in the new creation. This truth is drawn out in two parallel utterances: "Whoever believes in me, even though he dies, will come to life"; i.e., the believer who dies will rise for life in the kingdom of God; it is a future resurrection. Then follows the affirmation, "Whoever lives and believes in me will never, never die." The expression, "whoever lives and believes" can hardly mean, "every person who is alive and believes," for nobody can believe except those who are alive. It must surely mean, "Everyone believing in me has the life of the saving sovereignty of God." Such a person will never, never "die"; that is, death cannot harm the life of one who has entered into the kingdom of eternal life. Thus John 11:25 is a double affirmation: first, by the power of him who is the Resurrection and the Life, the believer will "live" after death; the believer will rise to life in the consummated sovereignty of God. Secondly, the believer who through faith possesses the life of the saving sovereignty has life which death cannot touch. The participation in the glorious future ordained by God is confirmed by participation in the eschatological reality of life through Christ.

(6) The same message is repeatedly affirmed in the discourse on the Bread of Life in chapter 6. It is most succinctly stated in 6:40: "This is my Father's will, that everyone who sees the Son and believes in him should have eternal life, and I shall raise him on the last day." The basis of this and similar utterances is stated in 6:57: "Just as the living Father sent me and I live because of the Father, so whoever eats me will live because of me." The relation to Christ of the believer who so "eats" the living Bread is analogous to the relation of the Son to the Father: as the Son lives "through the Father," i.e., has his life from and is sustained by the Father, so the believer has his or her life from and is sustained by the Son. This is the conse-

quence for humanity of the Son acting as the mediator between God and humankind.

(7) Here is the final meaning of Peter's declaration of faith to Jesus: "You have the words of eternal life" (6:68). The words of Jesus assure those who receive them of the abundant life of the kingdom of God, in this world and in the world to come.

From the foregoing it is evident that, as Mussner observed, "life" is "the comprehensive concept of salvation which contains everything that the Savior of the world, sent by God, brings to man." His exposition of that affirmation, made in light of his investigation of life in the Fourth Gospel, is noteworthy, and I take leave to cite it:

> To it (viz., the concept of life in John) belongs the transition from death to "life"; preservation from the judgment of death; rescue from *apoleia*, i.e., eternal ruin; emancipation from the rule of the "prince of this world"; possession of the Spirit who makes alive; becoming a child of God through the "begetting from God"; fellowship with the glorified Christ and through him with the Father, now in the earthly life and one day in a perfect manner in the Father's house; enjoyment of the love of God; joy and peace, possession of the "light"; the "knowledge" of God; participation in the *doxa*, the glory of Christ, and beholding it in the heavenly world; likeness to the glorified, heavenly Son of Man, and guarantee of the resurrection to life through him on the last day. According to the Johannine conception there are not blessings of salvation which are given to the believer in addition to the saving gift of "life"; the remaining gifts of salvation are given and guaranteed along with the "life," whether for the present or for the eschatological future. Hence the Johannine Christ can proclaim that he has come "that they may have life, and have it in fulness" (10:10), and that the commission for man laid upon him by the Father is simply "eternal life" (12:50).[10]

That expresses admirably the truth about "life" in the Gospel of John. To know it and experience it is God's offer to every child of the human race. To proclaim it is our high privilege. The more profoundly we know it, and the more fully we experience it, the more effectively we shall make it known.

NOTES TO 1

1. F. Mussner, *Zōē, Die Anschauung vom "Leben" im vierten Evangelium*, Münchener theologische Studien, 1. Historische Abteilung, 5. Band, Munich: K. Zink Verlag, 1952, p. 178. The reference to A. Titius is to his book *Die neutestamentliche Lehre von der Seligkeit und ihre*

Bedeutung für die Gegenwart, part 3, Die Johanneische Anschauung unter dem Gesichtspunkt der Seligkeit, Tübingen 1900, p. 18.

2. R. Bultmann, *The Gospel of John,* trans. G. R. Beasley-Murray et al. Oxford: Blackwell, 1971, p. 431.

3. R. Bultmann, *Theology of the New Testament,* trans. K. Grobel, New York: Charles Scribner's Sons, 1951 and 1955, vol. 2, p. 57.

4. S. Schulz, *Das Evangelium nach Johannes,* NTD 4, Göttingen: Vandenhoeck & Ruprecht, pp. 220–22.

5. So W. G. Kümmel, *Promise and Fulfillment, The Eschatological Message of Jesus,* SBT 12, London: SCM, 1957, p. 155. See further idem, "Noch einmal: Das Gleichnis von der selbstwachsenden Saat," in *Orientierung an Jesus,* Festschrift for J. Schmid; ed. P. Hoffmann et al., Freiburg, 1971, p. 235.

6. G. Bertram, "*hypsoō, ktl,*" *TDNT,* vol. 8, p. 612.

7. W. Thüsing, *Erhöhungsvorstellungen und Parusieerwartung in der ältesten nachösterlichen Christologie,* Stuttgarte Bibelstudien 42, 1969, first published in *BZ NF* 95, vols. 11 and 12.

8. C. H. Dodd, *The Interpretation of the Fourth Gospel,* Cambridge: Cambridge University Press, 1953, p. 395.

9. Ibid.

10. Mussner, *Zōē,* pp. 186–87; trans. author.

CHAPTER 2

THE MISSION OF
THE SON OF GOD

IN HIS STUDY OF THE FOURTH GOSPEL from the vantage point of
John 17, E. Käsemann cited the aphorism of Count Nicholas
von Zinzendorf: "I have but one passion: that is he, only he."[1]
Zinzendorf, of course, was speaking of Jesus. The Fourth Evangelist could well have uttered that statement. The controlling
concern of his Gospel is Christology. All other theological con-
cerns, such as salvation, eschatology, Holy Spirit, church, and
world, are related to the one great theme. And it is a complex
theme. As J. D. G. Dunn remarked, it continues to tease and
test the minds of Christians still. "In a real sense," he added,
"the history of Christological controversy is the history of the
church's attempt to come to terms with John's Christology—
first to accept it, then understand and re-express it. *The latter
task will never end.*"[2]

A comparatively recent approach to understanding the issues and resolving the problems is expressed in the title of this
chapter. It attempts to take seriously the frequency within the
Gospel of the concept of the "sending" of the Son by the Father,
along with the acknowledged primacy of the concept of "Son"
among the christological titles in the Fourth Gospel.

A mere enumeration of the number of times that the sending of Jesus into the world occurs in the Gospel is striking.
Bultmann counted seventeen examples of the participial phrase
"he who sent me" (*ho pempsas me*), plus six occurrences of the
expression "the Father who sent me" (with the same verb); and
he noted fifteen corresponding statements in which the syn-

onymous verb *apostellein*, "send out," is used.[3] This phenomenon led Marinus de Jonge to observe, "No other single Christological expression appears so often in the Fourth Gospel."[4] The contrast with the infrequency of these expressions in the synoptic Gospels is quite extraordinary. Mark has no explicit example of the sending of Jesus, other than in the parable of the wicked tenant farmers to whom the landowner sends his son (Mark 12:6). Matthew has two instances (10:40; 15:24), with the passage in 10:40 being particularly important. Luke has *none* of his own tradition, but he does include the text of Jesus' sermon in the synagogue of Nazareth, Isaiah 61:1-2a:

> The Spirit of the Lord is upon me, because he anointed me to preach the gospel to the poor. He has sent me to proclaim release to the captives, and recovery of sight to the blind, to set free those who are downtrodden, to proclaim the acceptable year of the Lord (Luke 4:18-19).

To ensure that we know what is being talked about, let me cite a few examples of the "sending" sayings in John's Gospel.

> If God were your Father you would love me, for I came forth from God and here I am; for I have not come of my own accord, but he sent me (John 8:42).

> The one whom God sent speaks the words of God, for he does not give the Spirit in a limited measure [to him] (3:34).

> My food is to do the will of him who sent me and to accomplish the work he gave me to do (4:34).

> I have greater witness than John's, for the works bear witness about me that the Father has sent me. And the Father who sent me has borne witness concerning me; his voice you have never heard, nor do you believe the one whom he sent (5:36-38).

The question arises as to the background and presuppositions of the concept of the mission of Jesus that is expressed in these and the many other similar sayings. E. Haenchen believed that according to the evangelist, God and his action are completely hidden, as the last sentence of the prologue indicates:

> Nobody has ever seen God at any time; the only Son, by nature God, has made him known (1:18).

Haenchen continued,

> Admittedly John does not affirm, as the Gnostics, that the world has arisen through a fall away from God, and that man must again

become conscious of his divinity. On the contrary, the universe has been made through the Logos, the mediator of creation. But the world of mankind which belongs to the Logos wishes to know nothing of him; it remains wrapped up in itself (it seeks only its own glory!). The world, this world, thus is incapable of pressing forward out of itself to God—especially if it thinks that it knows him already (8:41). According to John there is only one possibility of obtaining knowledge of the Father, namely if he sends someone with such knowledge. With that we reach the problem of Johannine christology, the most important of all Johannine problems. As John himself came to understand it is set forth in the ever repeated formula, "the Father who has sent me." Jesus is the One sent by the Father.[5]

There is truth in this statement, inasmuch as blindness and resistance to the ministry of the Logos on the part of humanity are plainly stated in the prologue (1:5, 10), and the need of people to be drawn by God to the Christ whom he has sent is later acknowledged (6:44). But the positive aspect is also recognized: the Logos is the life and light of humankind, both in creation and in redemption (1:4), and there have always been those who have responded to his ministry (1:12). Moreover the statement in 1:18, "No man has ever seen God," should be set in its context; in it a contrast is drawn between Moses and Jesus. Moses requested to see God's glory, but he was allowed to see only God's back, for in the narrative of Exodus 33 alluded to, no one can see God's face and live! Nevertheless out of the fellowship with God that was given to Moses, the divine law was mediated to the people of God. The contrast in 1:18, accordingly, is not between total ignorance of God and the revelation conveyed through God's Son, but between the partial glimpses of God given to the prophets, including Moses, and the full revelation that issued from him who is "in the bosom of the Father." Out of that association of the Son with the Father, the Son of God was sent forth to make God fully known.

In contrast to the restricted view of Haenchen, J. A. Bühner has written a classic study of the sending of Christ in the Fourth Gospel. He pointed out that humanity as a social being has always wanted possibilities of sending news to others and has arranged for that to come to pass. It was the most natural thing in the world to apply this idea to the relations between God (or the gods!) and humanity, and God's communications with humanity. So arose the concept of the prophet as a messenger of God, and the concept of angels as messengers sent from heaven to humankind. This concept was so pervasive in the ancient orient that it was adopted by adherents of many religions, including Semitic and Greek forms of religion. This needs to be remembered in the much discussed matter of the relation of the messenger of God in the Fourth Gospel with the Gnostic myth of the Revealer who descends from heaven and ascends thither. The latter was but one example among many of the adaptation of the concept of the messenger of God (or the gods); it did not require dependence of one particular religion on another for its adoption. Jews and Greeks, non-Christian and Christian, drew upon an all but universal social convention, that of the messenger.[6]

It is commonly recognized among scholars who have written on this issue that there were three basic elements in the ancient messenger procedures: (1) the giving of news by the person who sent the messenger; (2) the carrying out of the task by the one sent; (3) the return of the messenger to the person who sent him, especially for the purpose of report. The same procedure applied if it were a task to be performed instead of news to be conveyed. In this process two important corollaries are to be noted: first, the messenger is viewed as the representative of the sender; second, obedience on the part of the messenger is demanded. The two thoughts are closely related. Only on the basis of the assumed obedience of the messenger is it possible to view the messenger as the representative of the sender, but when that is accepted the messenger's word may be received as the word of the sender. The combination of the two assumptions supplies the messenger with credibility, legitimacy, and authority. This position is embodied in the famous statement of Jewish halachic law: "One sent is as he who sent him." The messenger is thereby granted authority and dignity by virtue of his bearing the status of the one who sent him. This is the more remarkable when it is borne in mind that in earlier times the messenger was commonly a slave. Such a person, however, belonged to the house of his master, and the honor and esteem in which the household was held were represented by the slave. Bühner described this identification as "socio-ontological," that is, grounded in the culture of that time. The messenger was identified with his master's "house," and the "house" was an extension of the master's personality, so that in his messenger, the sender himself acted.[7] The contacts be-

tween these ideas and the depictions in the Fourth Gospel of
Jesus as the One sent by God will be immediately apparent.

(1) The fundamental fact that God sent Jesus into the world
is stated by the evangelist time and again. Frequently this sending is merely referred to in passing, but the very constancy of
its mention indicates how deeply the thought is rooted in the
Gospel, not to say in the Lord's mind. For example, when objection is made to Jesus' being the Messiah, on the grounds that
people know where he is from, whereas the Messiah's origin is
unknown (a reference to the doctrine of the hidden Messiah),
Jesus answers:

> You both know me and know where I come from. I have not come
> of my own accord, but the one who sent me is true, and him you
> do not know; but I know him, because *I am from him, and he it is*
> *who sent me* (7:28–29).

Again, when Jewish opponents of Jesus claimed that Abraham
was their earthly father and God their Father in heaven, Jesus
replied,

> If God were your Father you would love me, for I have come from
> God and here I am; for I have not come of my own accord, but *he*
> *sent me* (8:42).

So also when Jesus expounds the enigmatic Psalm 82:6: "I said
'You are gods, and all of you are sons of the Most High God,' "
which both he and his hearers took to be addressed to God's
people, he asks,

> Do you say regarding the one whom the Father *consecrated and*
> *sent into the world,* "You are blaspheming," because I said, "I am
> the Son of God"? (John 10:36).

It will be observed that certain of these passages betray a silent
transition from the simple thought of Jesus' being "sent" to the
more profound thought of his being sent in incarnation.

(2) The same ambiguity occurs in passages that refer to
Jesus' being sent with a message from God. In 3:34 the evangelist makes the general observation, "The one whom God sent
speaks the words of God," which in the context plainly refers
to Jesus; and so he adds, "for he does not give the Spirit in a
limited measure to him." Thus the authority as well as the
fact of Jesus' being sent is asserted here. The same is stated
in John 17:8:

I have given them the words that you gave to me, and they have received them and come to know in truth that I came forth from you, and *they have believed that you have sent me* (see also 17:25–26).

(3) The messenger is sometimes sent in order to perform a task rather than to convey a message. Such we find in the Gospel. There are passages which simply affirm that the Son of God is sent to do works on behalf of the Father. In 5:36, for example, Jesus declares,

The works which the Father has given me to achieve, the very works that I do bear witness concerning me that the Father has sent me.

Sometimes the words and the works given to Jesus to say and to do are conjoined to emphasize the importance of their testimony. In the Upper Room discourse Philip asks Jesus to show them the Father. Jesus' reply is well known:

Have I been so long a time with you and you have not come to know me, Philip? Anyone who has seen me has seen the Father. You do believe, don't you, that I am in the Father and the Father is in me? The *words* that I am telling you all I am not speaking of my own accord; but it is the Father dwelling in me who is doing his *works*. Believe me that I am in the Father and the Father is in me, otherwise believe because of the works themselves (14:9–11).

The implication of the passage will not go unnoticed. Similarly the words and the works of Jesus have been given to Jesus to say and do; accordingly they are the Father's words and works—he is doing them through Jesus. This shows that the Father and Jesus are "in" each other, hence to see Jesus is to see the Father. Representation of the sender by the messenger here reaches its apex.

The same kind of concept is expressed in different terms in that very significant passage, 5:19–30. In answer to the Jewish accusation that in calling God his own Father Jesus was making himself equal to God, Jesus declares:

The Son can do nothing by himself, only what he sees the Father doing; for what he does, the Son does likewise. For the Father loves the Son and shows him everything that he himself does, and he will show him greater works than these that you may be amazed.

Far from claiming equality with God, Jesus asserts that the Son can do *nothing* of himself but is wholly dependent on the Father to accomplish the works that he shows him to do. But the scope of the works is breathtaking. The "greater works" referred to by Jesus include giving life to the dead and executing the judgment of God.

> As the Father raises the dead and gives them life, so also the Son gives life to those whom he wishes. The Father judges no one, but he has given all judgment to the Son, so that all should honor the Son, just as they honor the Father.

Here the *shaliach* principle, "One sent is as he who sends him," reaches extraordinary heights: people are to give the same honor to the Son as they give to the Father. But more follows. The giving of life and passing of judgment are explicitly related to humankind in the present.

> He who hears my word and believes on him who sent me has eternal life; he does not come to judgment but has crossed over from death to life.

That happens through hearing the word of the messenger Son and believing in the Father. But the text continues with assigning the functions of raising the dead and passing judgment to the Son, both in the present and in the future:

> The hour is coming and now is when the dead will hear the voice of the Son of God, and they who hear will live. For just as the Father has life in himself, so also he has granted the Son to have life in himself; and he gave him authority to pass judgment, because he is the Son of Man.

(4) These utterances reach their climax in the declarations that the Son has been sent into the world to bring salvation to humanity. It finds unforgettable expression in John 3:16–17, where the messenger concept is first affirmed in the words, "God *gave* his Son, . . ." and then is explicitly stated in v. 17, "For God did not *send* the Son into the world to condemn the world, but that the world might be saved through him." The "giving" of the Son embraces both his incarnation and his vicarious death; he is given *to* the world and *for* the world; hence the entire mission of the Son for the redemption of the world is in view. On this Bultmann commented:

> The mission of the Son, embracing as it does both his humiliation and his exaltation, is of decisive importance, for it is by faith in this mission that man gains life.

> This means that the mission is the *eschatological event*, as the present tense *echei* ("has") in v. 15 indicates, and as vv. 17–21 expressly state. In this event the judgment of the world takes place.[8]

The discourse on the Bread of Life in chapter 6 sets forth the same teaching under a quite different image. The discourse is sparked off by the "sign" of the feeding of the multitude, but it reaches its heart through the contrast between the manna that came down from heaven during the time of Moses and the bread that the one greater than Moses gives. The Jews anticipated that the Messiah would restore the manna in the time of the kingdom of God: "As the First Redeemer brought down the manna . . . so will the Last Redeemer cause the manna to come down (*Midr. Qoh.* 1a). Jesus states, however, that the Father, who gave the manna in the wilderness, gives the true bread from heaven, and that is none other than himself. This affirmation is expounded in terms of the messenger's task assigned by the Father:

> I have come down from heaven not to do my own will but the will of him who sent me; and this is the will of him who sent me: that I should lose nothing of what he has given me, but raise it on the last day. For this is my Father's will that everyone who sees the Son and believes in him should have eternal life, and I shall raise him on the last day (John 6:38–40).

Thus the power and authority of the Son to give life to the world derives from his commission from the Father who sent him for this purpose.

(5) It will be recalled that obedience is a prime requisite in one sent as a messenger. Only when the trustworthiness of a messenger can be relied on is it possible to receive the messenger as the representative of the sender. This element of the role of Jesus as the messenger of God appears in not a few passages in the Gospel. It is expressed in a general sense, without any polemic, in the utterance of Jesus to his disciples, John 4:34:

> My food is to do the will of him who sent me and to accomplish the work he gave me to do.

This suggests not simply an awareness of Jesus that he is called to be obedient to the Father's will, but a devotion to it and an enthusiasm for it that takes precedence over even the natural necessities of the body. In 5:30 Jesus repeats what he said earlier: "I can do nothing by myself," but he continues with a fresh thought:

> It is as I hear that I judge, and my judgment is just, because I do not seek my own will, but the will of him who sent me.

There may well be here a hint of polemic against those who oppose the claim of Jesus to have authority to judge. He states that he has no such power in himself; it is "as he hears" that he judges, namely, as he hears the decisions of his Father, who appointed him to be his representative in judgment. Such judgments are "just," he adds, because "I do not seek my will, but the will of him who sent me." That applies to his judgments every day and the last day.

Perhaps the most dramatic example of Jesus' consciousness that he must obey the Father's will occurs in the last sentence of the Wrst Upper Room discourse (14:31). The translation is uncertain. We may render it:

> The world must know that I love the Father and do just as the Father commanded me. Rise up, let us go from this place.

Or we may translate:

> In order that the world may know that I love the Father and do just as the Father commanded me, rise up, let us go from this place!

While Jesus is concerned that all should know that he does the will of the Father *always*, he undeniably has a specific command to obey in this situation, and that is why he and his disciples must "rise up and go." Where are they going? To meet Judas and the soldiers and the police on their way to arrest him, to confront Annas and Caiaphas and Pilate for his trial, to walk along the road that leads to Golgotha and there lay down his life for the sake of the world. We are reminded of the famous cry of the Duke of Wellington at Waterloo: "Up guards, and at 'em!" In such a manner Jesus rises to fulfill the Father's commission to deliver the world from its destruction for life in the kingdom of God.

(6) In all the varied aspects of the commission of Jesus to act as the messenger of God we have noticed the *authority* with which he is invested. It is necessary, however, to state this feature explicitly, since it is basic to the whole concept of sending. Whether it be the fulfillment of Jesus' task to declare the revelation from the Father, or to work the works of God that manifest his kingdom, or to walk obediently in the path of the Father's will, or to lay down his life in order to take it again for the salvation of the world, in all these aspects of his calling Jesus acts with the authority given by the Father who sent him. This

is made plain in the evangelist's conclusion to the public ministry of Jesus in John 12:44–50. The passage is composed of words of Jesus that summarize the proclamation he has made to his people and therefore to the world. Significantly the summary is dominated by the theme of the sending of Jesus into the world, the reality of his representation of God, and the authority of his message and mission. So we read:

> Jesus cried out and said: "He who believes in me does not simply believe in me but in the One who sent me, and he who sees me sees the One who sent me. . . . He who sets me aside and does not receive my words has his judge: the word that I have spoken will judge him in the last day; for I have not spoken on my own authority, but the Father who sent me has given me a command what to say and what to speak. And I know that his command means life eternal. What therefore I speak, I speak just as the Father has told me."

(7) Not infrequently Jesus declares his assurance that in all his ministry the Father is with him. The best known example of this is his statement to the disciples in the Upper Room that they will all forsake him and leave him alone, but—"I am not alone, for the Father is with me" (16:32). In the controversial dialogue of chapter 8 this is linked with the sending motif, almost certainly because of the recognized solidarity of the sender with his messenger. In the Old Testament this is often applied to the actual presence of God with his representatives. So at the sending of Moses in the theophany of the burning bush, the Lord says,

> Come now, and I will send you to Pharaoh, so that you may bring my people, the sons of Israel, out of Egypt.

When Moses protests:

> Who am I that I should go to Pharaoh, and that I should bring the sons of Israel out of Egypt?

the Lord replies, "*Certainly I will be with you*" (Exod. 3:10–12). So we find Jesus saying,

> He who sent me is with me; he has not left me alone, because I always do the things that are pleasing to him (John 8:29).

We observed earlier that Jesus acknowledged that he could do nothing by himself, let alone judge the world, but he added, "It is *as I hear* that I judge"; i.e., he judges as he hears the Father's instructions (5:30). That is more vividly brought out in 8:16:

Even if I do judge, my judgment is authentic, because it is not I alone who judges, but I and the Father who sent me.

The implications of that are far reaching: there is no activity of Jesus in which he acts alone; as the messenger of the Father and as his representative in the world, Jesus performed every action under the guidance and in the power of God.

(8) It must not go unnoticed that Jesus extends to his disciples the same commission that he has received from the Father, and he applies the same principles of sending to them. "Amen, amen I tell you, he who receives anyone I send receives me, and he who receives me receives the One who sent me" (13:20); the saying is closely paralleled in Matt. 10:40). This is the basis on which Jesus sent out his followers during his ministry, but in our Gospel the emphasis falls on the sending in the resurrection. Accordingly, in the Prayer of Consecration in chapter 17, Jesus prays, in light of his death and resurrection, "As you sent me into the world I also have sent them into the world; and for their sakes I consecrate myself, that they also may become consecrated in the truth" (vv. 18–19). The apostles are expected to undertake their mission in the same spirit of sacrifice that characterized his own path. And so the commission of the Risen Lord to his disciples is summarized in language similar to that in the prayer: "As the Father has sent me, I also am sending you" (20:21).

(9) Finally the messenger returns to the one who sent him. There is an early reference to this, spoken by Jesus in the temple during the Festival of Tabernacles:

> For a little longer time I am with you, and then I am going away to the One who sent me. You will look for me, but you will not find me, and where I am you are unable to come (7:33–34).

A much clearer reference to this event is made by the evangelist at the beginning of his account of the Last Supper:

> It was just before the Passover festival; Jesus, in full awareness that his hour had come that he should pass from this world to the Father, having always loved his own who were in the world he showed his love for them to the limit (13:1).

And again:

> Jesus, knowing that the Father had given all things into his hands, and that he had come from God and was going away to God, rises from the meal . . . (13:3–4).

The solemnity of the moment is emphasized by the evangelist, for it marked the beginning of his account of the "hour" which Jesus had anticipated so long; it was the hour when he would glorify God through his death for humankind and the hour which would mark his crossing over from this world to the Father's side (so 17:5).

This is the theme of the final prayer of Jesus. From first to last it is dominated by Jesus' consciousness that he has completed the commission given to him by the Father and that he is now to return to him. He therefore prays that the consecration of his life to death may be an acceptable sacrifice and that through it the Father may be glorified and the Son similarly glorified through exaltation to the Father's presence. He further prays for his disciples: "While I was with them I kept them in your name . . . but *now I am on my way to you*" (17:12–13). So also for the church that is to be he prays that all may be one in the holy fellowship with the Father *into which he is now again entering* (17:20–21, 22, 23).

(10) The suggestion has been put forward by Bühner that the "I am" sayings of the Fourth Gospel are to be viewed in light of the messenger concept. He points out that a messenger often introduces himself in a statement beginning with "I am," in a similar manner to those commencing with "I have come." In Genesis 24, for example, we read of Abraham's sending a servant to his distant relatives to bring from them a wife for Isaac. When he arrives he identifies himself, "I am Abraham's servant," and discloses the nature of his mission; when they agree to release Rebekah for Isaac he says, "Send me away to my master" (vv. 34, 54). Many such examples are to be found in Jewish literature—Bühner gives several pages of them. To cite a few: in Pesikta Rabbati 20, Moses says to Kemuel, who resists him from entering the heavenly realm: "I am the son of Amram, and have come to fetch the Torah for Israel." Abraham Bin Gorion has the statement: "My son, I am Elijah, and I have come to bring you news." From an account of Michael the archangel: "I am Michael, who receive your prayers and supplications and charities, and bring them up to God." As with the simple concept of the sender and his messenger, this mode of speech is in no way dependent on Hellenistic notions of the heavenly redeemer. It is a natural development of the sender-sent one concept. In this kind of self-introduction of a messen-

ger the basic form is "I am" plus a functional predicate. The predicate mediates between the commission, the messenger, and the message. As the functional idea of "apostle" (= messenger!) anticipates in a formal way the message of the messenger, so the predicate to "I am" receives a form of the message brought by the messenger, modified or specified according to content.[9]

That may appear an obscure explanation of an apparently simple usage, but it is evident that the message and the mission of Jesus (the messenger!) are distinctly set forth in the "I am" sayings of the Gospel. The first of these sayings is John 6:35: "I am the bread of life; he who comes to me will never again become hungry and he who believes in me will never again become thirsty." Significantly it finds repetition in a manner that specifically relates to the mission of the messenger:

> I am the living bread *which came down from heaven;* if anyone eats this bread he will live forever, and the bread which I shall give is my flesh, for the life of the world (6:51).

Similarly the well-known John 14:6, "I am the way, the truth and the life; no one comes to the Father except through me," follows a declaration of the mission of Jesus to open the way for humanity to live in the Father's house from which he came, and to which he is returning (14:2–4).

It is, of course, plain that the *absolute* "I am" sayings of Jesus (John 6:20; 8:24, 28, 58; 13:19) are not to be reckoned with sayings which have a predicate. They are, as Bühner acknowledges, revelations of the Christ. The most striking of these utterances is that which concludes the stormy controversy in chapter 8: "Before Abraham came into existence, *I am*" (8:58). The sentence contrasts created human life, even of the noblest order, with absolute existence. The precedent for this and the related sayings in the Gospel occurs in certain passages of Deutero-Isaiah,[10] notably Isaiah 43:10: "You are my witnesses, says the Lord . . . that you may know and believe me and understand that *I am he*" (literally "*I . . . he*"). This expression is equivalent to the assertion in the following verse, "I am the Lord." The Septuagint renders "I (am) he" by the simple *egō eimi,* i.e., "I am." Joseph Blank remarked on its application to Jesus in John 8:58 as implying: "Those who debate with Jesus have to do with the historical Revealer and Representative of Yahweh, and thus *with Yahweh himself.*" [11] This is not to assert that "I am" on the lips of Jesus signifies a direct identification of himself with God, but it is without doubt an affirmation in the strongest possible sense of the status of Jesus as the one sent by God to be his representative and the revealer of his word. As such it is a fresh expression of the Logos theology. It entails the unity of Jesus with the Father who sent him in a manner that transcends every human example of one sent with the one who sends him.

(11) In our discussions thus far of the mission of the Son we have virtually confined ourselves to sayings relating to the Father and *the Son.* There are, however, a number of crucially important utterances that concern the ministry of *the Son of Man.* How do they relate to the theme of the mission of the Son? First, it should be observed that the eschatological associations which are apparent in the synoptic Son of Man sayings hold true for the Johannine Son of Man statements as well. This is evident in the first of such utterances in our Gospel, namely, 1:51: "Amen, amen I say to you all: you will see heaven standing open, and the angels of God ascending and descending to the Son of Man." Commentators often call attention to the contacts of language and thought between this statement and the Markan sayings about the parousia of the Son of Man (Mark 8:38; 13:26; 14:62). Undoubtedly John 1:51 is an eschatological saying, but it relates to the *entire* ministry of Jesus, not only his signs (the first of which is recorded immediately following the saying), but to the whole sweep of his works, including his death and resurrection, all of which constitute the mediation of the divine sovereignty, the kingdom of God. But the most significant feature of the Son of Man sayings in the Fourth Gospel is their parallelism with those that concern the Son. There is an interpenetration of the mission of the Son with that of the Son of Man, and *it operates in both directions.* This appears most plainly in 5:17–29: *the Son* performs the works which the Father has continued from creation onward and which will reach their climax in the last day. These works include giving life and exercising judgment; in 5:27 the judgment is stated to be the prerogative of *the Son* "because he is *the Son of Man.*" In 3:14–15 *the Son of Man* is to be "lifted up" in order that all who believe may have in him eternal life; that is expounded in vv. 16–21 in terms of the sending of *the Son* for life and judgment. The reverse phenomenon is observable in 12:27–28, 31–34: *the*

Son undergoes a Gethsemane kind of agony in anticipation of his "hour"; that hour proves to be the hour of judgment and salvation, when the devil is dethroned and redemption is achieved for all humanity by *the Son of Man.* The works of the Son who is Son of Man are ultimately those of God through him; and so his unity with the Father is emphasized—in terms of *the Son* in 10:30 ("I and the Father are one") and in terms of *the Son of Man* in 8:28 ("When you have lifted up the Son of Man you will know that I am").

Some recent Johannine scholars have attempted to explain the relationship between the concepts "Son" and "Son of Man" in terms of a religious-historical development from a (comparatively) primitive concept of Son of Man to a more profound view of the Christ as the Son. It is postulated that early Johannine thought followed an early Christian view of the Son of Man as an apocalyptic figure, whose eschatological functions applied only to the end of the age. In due course, however, these were tempered to apply to a present realization of judgment and salvation. In Daniel, as elsewhere in Jewish apocalyptic, the Son of Man is an angelic figure, who descends from heaven to accomplish his eschatological tasks. It is urged that this understanding of the Son of Man will have been accepted by the Johannine community. In accordance with contemporary notions of prophetic ecstasy its members will have believed that Jesus, in ecstatic contemplation, ascended in vision into heaven and became one with, and so changed into, the Son of Man (cf. the like destiny of Enoch in the Similitudes). Hence the Son of Man descended to earth in the ministry of Jesus to reveal the heavenly world, as indicated in John 3:13, and ascended again through the death (= ascension) of Jesus (so John 3:13, 12:32). All this became transferred to the figure of the Son, and so arose the doctrine of incarnation.[12]

This is a highly speculative solution of a complex problem, and a highly doubtful one too. That the Son of Man of Daniel, together with the entire apparatus of the vision of Daniel 7, has an ancient history I do not doubt; but I do not believe that the author of that chapter viewed him and the monsters of the deep as angels; Antiochus Epiphanes was in view as the most monstrous of the monsters, and he was no angel! Nor is there any evidence that Jesus or his followers thought of the Son of Man as an angel. The transcendental eschatology of the Similitudes of Enoch is altogether different from that of Jesus and his church. That the Son of Man concept was important to Jesus is clear, precisely because the Son of Man is an eschatological figure, and Jesus came for an eschatological purpose, proclaiming and bringing the kingdom of God. But his consciousness of sonship to God will have been prior even to that (cf. *Abba*), and will have accounted for his understanding of his calling to be God's instrument in relation to the kingdom of God. The instinct of most students of John's Gospel is surely right: "The Father-Son relationship is the key to the understanding of Jesus as portrayed by the evangelist and of his words and actions as interpreted by him."[13]

One thing is surely evident in our survey of the sayings in John concerning the mission of Jesus: the mission originates with the sending by *the Father*, and the messenger is *the Son*. In a variety of ways, prompted by the varied aspects of the image of sender and messenger, the unity of the Father and the Son is set forth, so that to see the Son is to see the Father (14:9). In their mission action they are one (10:30, cf. vv. 27–29). That unity of action is rooted in a unity of holy fellowship, expressed in terms of the mutual indwelling of the Father and the Son ("I am in the Father, and the Father in me," 14:10).

With this the prologue to the Gospel is wholly in agreement. From the christological viewpoint it makes explicit what is implicit in the body of the Gospel. If it is true, as Floyd Filson argued, that the term "Logos" is used as an "attention catcher,"[14] then the theological importance of the prologue must not on that account be minimized.[15] It should be viewed rather, as H. Thyen affirmed, as "a directive to the reader how the entire gospel should be read and understood."[16] The prologue may be seen as an anticipatory description of the mission of the Logos-Son to the world, in preparation for the extended exposition of the theme in the Gospel. Creation came into being through the Logos; as the mediator of creation he continues to be the source of life among humankind; he is its "Light and Life" (1:4). Admittedly the language of John 1:4 is somewhat ambiguous, as also is that of vv. 9–12b; both passages can be related to the activity of the Logos prior to the incarnation, described in v. 14, and *also* to the incarnate ministry of the Son of God. Augustine, in a famous passage in his *Confessions*, described how he found everything contained in the first thirteen verses of the prologue in the writings of the Platonists.[17] There is little doubt that any non-Christian Platonist who chanced to read the prologue would have assumed that the universal work of the Logos in the world was the subject as far as v. 13; not until v. 14 would the non-Christian Platonist find any mention of the activities of the Logos *as man*. Nevertheless vv. 10–12b can be understood as a summary in retrospect of the ministry of Jesus, and vv. 12c–13 most naturally relate to the gospel of new life in Christ. C. H. Dodd was strongly of the opinion that this ambiguity of the text was intended by the evangelist. Non-Christian readers would understand the first thirteen verses of the prologue as describing the Logos of which they knew, and so they would receive the full impact of the astonishing news of v. 14, whereas Christians would perceive the fullest meaning of the latter half of the prologue in the incarnate Son. Dodd therefore urged:

> The whole passage from v. 4 is at once an account of the relations of the Logos in the world *and* an account of the ministry of Jesus Christ, which in every essential particular reproduces those relations.

This is possible on the ground that

> The life of Jesus is the history of the Logos as incarnate, and this must be, upon the stage of limited time, the same thing as the history of the Logos in perpetual relations with man and the world.[18]

We are led therefore to the conviction that the mission of the Logos-Son is a continuing one, reaching from the dawn of time and persisting till the incarnation and all that flowed from it. Verse 14 is the pivotal utterance of the prologue in relation to the mission of the Son of God, but the sayings that follow indicate that the "exposition" of the Father by "the only Son, by nature God" (v. 18) took place through the redemptive word and redemptive deed of Jesus (note the emphatic use of the term "grace" in vv. 14, 16, 17, which occurs only here in the Gospel). The nature of that redemptive word and deed the Gospel alone can make plain.

One final issue concerning the Christology of the Fourth Gospel needs to be faced in view of the widespread discussions on it, namely, whether the Gospel sets forth a *functional* or *ontological* understanding of Jesus; i.e., whether the evangelist viewed Jesus purely in terms of what he did as God's instrument for salvation, or whether he wished to convey a doctrine concerning the person of Jesus in relation to God. R. Kysar reviewed the efforts of four Johannine scholars to solve this problem (J. A. T. Robinson, J. Riedle, H. Schlier, and K. Haacker). He expressed his own conviction as follows:

> It is, at least in my opinion, more likely that the early Christian movement first rooted itself in an existential sense of what this

man Jesus had done in the lives of those who contacted him than it is to imagine the early emergence of a set of assertions about the identity and origin of this figure. The functions of the Christ figure could conceivably give rise to the assertions about his person; but the real function-person approach to the christology of the fourth gospel holds constantly before the interpreter the proper priority of function.[19]

One should note that while stressing the priority of function, Kysar acknowledged that function and person are not separable in the thought of the evangelist. That must be doubly emphasized. When one considers that the Fourth Gospel begins with a sentence that concludes with the affirmation, "and the Word was God," and when one observes that it reaches its climax in the confession of Thomas to the Risen Christ, "My Lord and my God" (20:28), it is consequently difficult to conclude that the evangelist in his exposition of Jesus in relation to God laid the emphasis on "the proper priority of function." We all acknowledge, of course, that John was concerned to make transparently plain the *action* of God in the whole mediatorial work of Jesus in bringing into being the new creation, that saving sovereignty we otherwise call the kingdom of God. For the evangelist, soteriology, eschatology, God's dealings with his people and with the world through Jesus, the mission of the Holy Spirit, the church, the sacraments, and the like are all set in relation to the Christ, the Son of God. How can the functions of the Christ be envisioned other than as expressive of his person? M. de Jonge remarked, "It does not make sense to play acting and being, function and nature, off against each other."[20] The majority of students of the Gospel agree.

In harmony with that conviction C. K. Barrett asserted: "John clarifies the relation of Jesus to God."[21] We concur. Such was the evangelist's intention, and such was his achievement.

NOTES TO 2

1. E. Käsemann, *The Testament of Jesus: A Study of the Gospel of John in the Light of Chapter 17*, trans. K. Grobel, London: SCM, 1968, p. 38.

2. J. D. G. Dunn, *Christology in the Making*, Philadelphia: Westminster, 1980, p. 250.

3. Bultmann, *Gospel of John*, p. 249, n. 2. Some writers have sought to establish a distinction of meaning between *pempein* and *apostellein* (so, e.g., K. Rengstorf, *apostellō* in *TDNT*, vol. 1, p. 404; J. Blank,

Krisis, Untersuchungen zur johanneischen Eschatologie, Freiburg: Lambertus, 1964, p. 36), even to the extent of distinguishing different sources in the Fourth Gospel through it (see, e.g., H. M. Teeple, *The Literary Origin of the Gospel of John,* Evanston: Religion & Ethics Institute, 1974, pp. 146–61). J. P. Miranda urges, surely rightly, that the two terms may be viewed as stylistic variants, as they are in John 20:21; if there is any difference *pempein* may bring to view the perspective of the sender and *apostellein* that of the one sent; see *Die Sendung Jesu im vierten Evangelium: Religions—und theologiegeschichtliche Untersuchungen zu den Sendungsformeln,* Stuttgart: Katholisches Bibelwerk, 1977, pp. 14–15.

4. M. de Jonge, *Jesus, Stranger from Heaven and Son of God,* Missoula: Scholars Press, 1977, p. 147.

5. E. Haenchen, "Der Vater der mich gesandt hat," *NTS* 9 (1963), p. 210.

6. J. A. Bühner, *Der Gesandte und sein Weg im 4. Evangelium,* WUNT, 2d Series, Tübingen: Mohr, 1977, pp. 118–21.

7. Ibid., pp. 124–25.

8. Bultmann, *Gospel of John,* p. 154.

9. Bühner, *Der Gesandte,* pp. 154–58.

10. So E. Zimmermann, "Das absolute *Egō eimi* als die neutestamentliche Offenbarungsformel," *BZ NF* (1960), pp. 54–69, 266–76! See also C. H. Dodd, *Interpretation,* pp. 93–96, 349–50; R. Schnackenburg, *The Gospel According to St. John,* New York: Crossroad, 1987, vol. 2, pp. 79–89.

11. Blank, *Krisis,* p. 246.

12. So Bühner, following the cue given by S. Schulz, *Das Evangelium nach Johannes,* pp. 110–17, and his *Untersuchungen zur Menschensohn-Christologie im Johannes-Evangelium.*

13. Schnackenburg, *Gospel According to St. John,* vol. 2, p. 172.

14. F. Filson, "The Gospel of Life: A Study of the Gospel of John," in *Current Issues in N. T. Interpretation: Feschrift O. A. Piper,* ed. W. Klassen and G. F. Snyder, New York: Harper, p. 111.

15. As when T. Preiss asserted that the prologue was "only a portal," not a key to the Gospel, *Life in Christ,* SBT 13, London: SCM, 1954, p. 10.

16. H. Thyen, "Aus der Literatur zum Johannesevangelium," *TR* 39 (1975) p. 223.

17. Augustine, *Confessions* 9.13, 14, translated by E. B. Pusey, London: Dent, 1907, pp. 129–31.

18. Dodd, *Interpretation,* p. 284.

19. R. Kysar, *The Fourth Evangelist and His Gospel: An Examination of Contemporary Scholarship,* Minneapolis: Augsburg Press, 1975, p. 204.

20. De Jonge, *Jesus Stranger from Heaven,* p. 150. See also Blank, *Krisis,* p. 36.

21. C. K. Barrett, *The Gospel According to St. John,* London: SPCK 1978, p. 54.

CHAPTER 3

THE LIFTING UP OF THE SON OF MAN

O UR BRIEF CONSIDERATION of the Gospel of John thus far has made it plain that its dominating motif is its Christology. The Gospel begins with an exposition of the incarnation of the Son of God in terms of the eternal Word of God made "flesh." It was perhaps inevitable that the overwhelming effect of the prologue should lead not a few theologians to believe that the death of Christ, which lies at the heart of the primitive preaching of the gospel, was displaced by the Christology of this Gospel and all but lost its significance.

This view was particularly common in the early part of this century. None other than so redoubtable an exponent of the death of Christ as James Denney was affected by this view. He wrote:

> The general conception of the fourth gospel is that what we owe to Christ is life, eternal life; and this life, it may further be said, we owe to the Person rather than to anything he does. This is true without any qualification of the prologue, and it is true of the gospel so far as the influence of the prologue can be traced through it. If we use the word redemption at all we must say that redemption is conceived in the gospel as taking place through revelation. Jesus redeems men, or gives them life, by revealing to them the truth about God. The revelation is made in his own Person—by his words and deeds, no doubt, but supremely by what he is. . . . The work of redemption, to borrow the dogmatic category, is interpreted through the prophetic office of Christ almost exclusively.[1]

One must add that Denney qualified this interpretation in light of the actual sayings on the death of Christ in the Gospel, which he saw as relatively unaffected by the Logos doctrine of the prologue.

E. F. Scott, in his work on the theology of the Fourth Gospel, followed more candidly the contemporary line. "The doctrinal import of the death of Christ," he wrote,

> is largely absorbed by John into his conception of a descent of the eternal Logos. . . . His appearance in the flesh constituted his sacrifice. The death at the close could not add to it anything that was essential.[2]

Bultmann expressed the same conviction in the language of a later generation: "Though for Paul, the incarnation of Christ is a part of the total salvation-occurrence, for John it is the decisive salvation-event."[3] Bultmann's one-time pupil and colleague, Ernst Käsemann, walked in the same path, though fortified with other considerations. For him the key to the exposition of the incarnation in the prologue was the clause, "We beheld his glory." And so he affirmed:

> In John the glory of Jesus determines his whole presentation so thoroughly from the very outset that the incorporation and position of the passion narrative becomes problematical. . . . One is tempted to regard it as being a mere postscript, which had to be included because John could not ignore this tradition, nor yet could he fit it organically into his work.[4]

Yet more recently, writers on John's Gospel have been taken up with the twofold theme of the descent and ascent of the Son of God and the representation of his death in terms of exaltation and glorification. Godfrey Nicholson, in a useful work devoted to this theme, came to the conclusion:

> The ambiguous "lift up" (*hypsoun*) occurs in contexts which are concerned with the descent and ascent of Jesus. . . . In such a context the word is used primarily to speak of Jesus being lifted up to the Father, and only on a secondary level to speak of the crucifixion-death of Jesus as the means by which this is accomplished.[5]

In the face of such views Marianne Meye Thompson tersely stated, "Glorification entails death; exaltation implies the cross," and she went on to cite Hoskyns:

> It is not that at the mention of death he (the evangelist) hurries on to speak of exaltation, but that when events might lead him to speak directly of Christ's glory he obstinately refers to his death.[6]

It is my intention in this chapter to pay special attention to the significance of those sayings which speak of the "lifting up" of Jesus, but not to the exclusion of the many other references to the Lord's death in the Gospel. We shall consider the latter first, and conclude with the crucifixion-exaltation-glorification sayings.

(1) The first reference to the death of Jesus in the Fourth Gospel is the witness of John the Baptist, recorded in John 1:29 and 36: "Look, the Lamb of God, who takes away the sin of the world." There is, of course, no actual mention of the death of Jesus in that saying, but it led to an artistic tradition through the centuries of John the Baptist depicted as a man carrying a cross, the cross of Jesus. I am persuaded, however, that the thought of a crucified messiah never entered John's mind, and that the evangelist knew that perfectly well.

In the Testaments of the Twelve Patriarchs, a Jewish apocalyptic work of uncertain date, there are two passages in which a portrayal of a "Lamb of God" is present. The image entails the thought of Israel as the flock of God. Israel is attacked by wild beasts of the earth, i.e., Gentile nations, and the sheep cry out for deliverance. In the Testament of Joseph 19:8f. a lion and a lamb appear, the former representing the kingly Messiah from Judah and the latter the priestly Messiah from Aaron. The text states:

all the beasts rushed against him (i.e., the lamb), and the lamb overcame them, and destroyed them, and trod them underfoot. And because of him, angels and men and all the earth rejoiced. . . . His kingdom is an everlasting kingdom, which shall not pass away (see also Testament of Benjamin 3).

Here is a purely apocalyptic picture of a lamb who delivers God's people, destroys their enemies (which are God's enemies), and enables the kingdom of God to be established. If it did not originate among the Qumran community it certainly was adopted by them. We recall that John the Baptist conducted his ministry not far from Qumran. That the Johannine churches knew of this concept is plain from the book of Revelation. In Revelation 5 the Christ is depicted as the conquering Lion of Judah who has thereby won the right to open the book that symbolizes God's covenant in order to give the kingdom to humanity. The figure of the Lion, however, is replaced by that of a slain Lamb who *stands,* i.e., is alive from the dead; he is the one who takes the book from God, and all heaven celebrates the event: "You were slaughtered and redeemed humankind to God by your blood from every tribe and tongue and people and nation. . . ." It used to be common to speak of the paradox of the Lion who is a Lamb, but they are parallel, not contrasting figures. The Lamb is not a weak, cuddly creature, crying for its mother, as British choirs love to sing.[7] He has *seven horns,* a symbol for the immense strength by which he can fight and destroy the beasts of the earth. He is, in fact, a super-powerful *ram!* But he has to be presented as a lamb, not as a lion, for he stands as one that has been *slaughtered,* and so he is a sacrificial victim risen from death; a dead lion plays no such role in Scripture (contrary to C. S. Lewis, with regrets!).

It is evident, accordingly, that in the book of Revelation an originally apocalyptic portrayal of the Messiah has been transformed through the Christian doctrine of redemption: the almighty Christ has won salvation for the world through his sacrificial death and resurrection. Precisely the same transformation has taken place in John 1:29. John the Baptist identifies Jesus as the mighty Lamb of God, whose task is to bring about the judgment of the wicked and the cleansing of the earth, and to enable the righteous to enter the kingdom of God (cf. Matt. 3:7–12). His witness is preserved unchanged in the Johannine community, but its interpretation is modified in light of the cross of Jesus and Easter: the Lamb of God brings deliverance through his sacrificial death and resurrection for life with the Father in heaven.

Can we say under what form the Lamb is viewed as a sacrifice? Yes, almost certainly as God's Passover Lamb. Of this we may be confident, not least because the typology of redemption as the second Exodus is prominent in both the Fourth Gospel and the book of Revelation (in the latter case it dominates the book from beginning to end). More specifically, I am persuaded that the evangelist wished us to interpret the witness of John in light of the incident narrated in John 19:31–37, just as the latter is to be interpreted in light of the witness of John in 1:29. In John 19:31–37 we are informed that late on the day of the preparation of the Passover Jewish leaders requested that the three crucified men on Golgotha have their legs broken and thereby be speedily put to death and be buried, so that the

land should not be defiled during the Passover (cf. Deut. 21:23).
Those leaders obviously knew the procedure: Roman soldiers
used to smash the legs of crucified men with an iron mallet,
virtually pulverizing them, so causing great loss of blood and
asphyxia, and leading to instant death. This the appointed soldiers did to the two criminals on either side of Jesus, and ad-
vancing on Jesus to do the same, they saw that he was dead
already; therefore, instead of smashing his legs, one of them
thrust a lance into his side—presumably to ensure that he really
was dead. This event greatly impressed the evangelist:

> The man who saw has borne witness, and his witness is authentic,
> and he knows that he tells the truth, that you, too, may believe.
> These events happened in order that the scripture might be ful-
> filled, "Not a bone of his is to be broken." And again another scrip-
> ture says, "They will look on him whom they pierced."

The latter citation is Zechariah 12:10. The first one occurs no
less than three times in the Old Testament: Exodus 12:46, Numbers 9:12, and Psalm 34:20. The first two give instructions as to
how the Passover meal should be eaten: not a bone of the lamb
is to be broken; the last one speaks of God's care for the suffering Righteous One, in that not one of his bones is broken. Both
applications were important to the primitive churches, but in
view of the emphasis of the evangelist on Jesus' being condemned and crucified at the time of the slaughter of the Passover lambs, there is little doubt that he would have seen in the
remarkable circumstance of Jesus' being preserved from being
"broken" a sign of the fulfillment of the Passover in his death.[8]
The frequently voiced objection to this interpretation, that the
Passover lamb was not viewed by the Jews as a sacrifice, is quite
mistaken. Without question the Passover lambs were slaughtered by the priests in the temple and thus tended increasingly
to be viewed as sacrificial victims. Moreover, because of Jewish
reflection on the meaning of the Passover, the sacrificial nature
of the blood of the Passover lamb came to be viewed as axiom-
atic. It was even appealed to in support for viewing the blood
of circumcision as sacrificial. G. Vermes stated:

> The sacrificial significance of circumcision is confirmed by the tra-
> ditional parallelism of this blood and the blood of the paschal lamb.
> According to the ancient teaching, the first Passover in the desert
> was celebrated by the mingling of the blood of both. Hence Lev.

17:11, "For the life of the flesh is in the blood" is paraphrased: "Life is in the blood of the Passover; life is in the blood of circumcision."[9]

It is evident, then, that the additional clause in John 1:29, "who takes away the sin of the world," is entirely in harmony with a Jewish as well as a Christian understanding. The thought of the fulfillment of Passover in relation to the concept of the second Exodus would lead to interpreting the death of Jesus in terms of "redemption." It is not to be ruled out, however, that since the thought of the Lamb of God taking away the sin of the world was a community tradition, shared by and not invented by the evangelist, other elements of the Jewish and Christian traditions could have been linked with this figure, notably the lamb provided by God at the intended sacrifice of Isaac (Gen. 22:10–19) and the submissive lamb of Isaiah 53. The former was of particular importance to Jews, who believed that all the sacrifices offered on the altar in the temple were acceptable to God by virtue of Abraham's "sacrifice" of Isaac. Just as various streams of thought flow together in the concept of the Word of God in the prologue, a similar development could have taken place with this, the first and crucially significant witness in the Gospel to the redemptive death of Jesus.

(2) John 3:16, "the gospel in a nutshell," is perhaps the most frequently quoted text of the Bible when Christians try to explain the essence of the Christian faith. It is also a profound theological utterance. Along with the statements that follow in vv. 17–21, it looks back on the life of Jesus in its totality and declares the purpose of it all. The saying is not represented as an utterance of Jesus, but is a declaration that summarizes the meaning of his life. In this respect it is to be compared with the brief statements of the kerygma and the confessions of faith that are found in the letters of the New Testament (e.g., Rom. 1:3–4; 3:25; 4:25; 10:9; 1 Cor. 15:3–4; 2 Cor. 5:19–20, etc.). In John 3:16 the gospel is stated to have its origin in the love of God for a disobedient world; it centers in the "giving" of the only Son of God—to and for the world—and its purpose is that people may not be lost, but live under the eternal, saving sovereignty of God. The "giving" of the only Son includes his incarnation and his vicarious death; the entire mission of the Son from heaven is in view. The suggestion has been made that the language deliberately echoes Abraham's *giving* his *only son,*

Isaac, whom he *loved* (Gen. 22:1–14; cf. Rom. 8:32, where the "giving up" of the only Son of God in death is compared with the readiness of Abraham to offer his only son, from which, however, God spared him, while not sparing himself). If the comparison was in mind, the actuality is much more vast. Here alone in the Fourth Gospel is the love of God for a rebellious world asserted to be the reason for the life and death of Christ (more commonly, love for the disciples of Jesus and the evil of the world are emphasized). But its uniqueness is no reason for diminishing the importance of the statement; it is the fundamental summary of the message of this Gospel, and it should therefore be viewed as a background of the canvas on which the rest of the Gospel is painted. We further need to ponder that people should not be "lost" but should receive the life of the eternal kingdom of God. That "lostness" has relation to the judgment of God, which elsewhere is characterized as the "wrath" of God (John 3:36). There is involved here a deeply serious view of the gravity of sin that called for such a mission of the Son of God to save humanity from it, and a deeply serious view of the relation of the Son's death to the judgment of God on sin.

The possibility of two destinies for humanity, lostness and life, is expounded in the immediately following sentences, and as Bultmann remarked, the love of God stands behind both.[10] It is the positive purpose of the mission of the Son that finds emphasis in v. 17. The incarnation, death, and resurrection of the Son of God took place so that all humankind might be saved. Since, however, this salvation is "in the Son" (v. 15) and gained through faith in him (v. 16), the sending of the Son can be turned into an occasion of judgment. That is the tragedy of the gospel: to spurn the love that went to the limit in seeking to save is to experience it as wrath.

The discourse on the Bread of Life in John 6 is related to the two signs narrated at the beginning of the chapter, the feeding of the multitude and the walking on the water. The statement about the nearness of the Passover in v. 4 is more than a mere date. Linked with the identification of Jesus as the prophet who would come as the eschatological successor to Moses (Deut. 18:15), and coupled with the comparison of the manna in the wilderness with the bread from heaven that Jesus gives (John 6:31–33), the whole scene becomes associated with the thought of the second Exodus. The feeding miracle is further viewed as an anticipation of the feast of the kingdom of God, as is the changing of the water into wine. On that basis the eschatological significance of the sign and its exposition in the discourse are doubly emphasized. Moreover, the sign's connection with the Lord's Supper, which again, is fundamentally linked with the kingdom of God, is additionally underscored.

But what does this have to do with the death of Jesus? The assertion in v. 35 that Jesus is the Bread of Life has itself no necessary connection with redemptive death. Jewish teachers often spoke of the law as bread and as easily identified the same with the manna given in the wilderness. It is as we progress through the discourse that we see how the life that Jesus bestows flows from redemptive action. "This is my Father's will, that everyone who sees the Son and believes in him should have eternal life, and I shall raise him on the last day" (v. 40). On the analogy of John 3:16, the faith in the Son that gains eternal life depends on the giving of the Son—for life and for death. And so we read in 6:51: "I am the living bread which came down from heaven; if anyone eats this bread he will live forever; and the bread that I shall give is my flesh—given for the life of the world." The bread is spoken of as "flesh" rather than "body," in part through reminiscence of John 1:14 (the Word became "flesh"), but still more to strengthen the sacrificial associations of the terms "give" and "on behalf of." The statement of 6:51 thus becomes a strong assertion of the sacrificial death of Jesus for the sake of humankind.

The use of the term *hyper*, "on behalf of," in connection with the death of Jesus here is noteworthy and is in harmony with its use elsewhere in the Gospel. In 10:11, 15, the death of Jesus is on behalf of the flock of God; in 11:50–52, on behalf of the Jewish people, and then, by implication, on behalf of the nations; in 17:19 it is on behalf of the disciples. If the evangelist intended that his readers should recall the Passover context throughout the entire chapter (6:4), then he would have wanted them to understand that he who is the Bread of Life is to die as the Lamb of God for the sake of the sin of the world (1:29). It has, however, been pointed out that in John 6 the Living Bread is said to give his flesh for the *life* of the world, not for its *sins*. But we have already recalled the sacrificial language of v. 51. Bread of Life for the *life* of the world is perfectly comprehensible; it is the theme of the whole chapter. But "life" for the world means eternal life under the saving sovereignty of God. The gift of life under that saving sovereignty has been at enormous cost, the Father's "giving" of the only Son for life and for death, and that is well represented in John 6:51. In the evangelist's mind the death of the Son of God for the life of the world has the dimensions of John 3:16. The sacramental implications of this teaching, as set forth in John 6, will be considered in chapter 6.

The discourse on the Shepherd and his flock (10:1–18) commences with a short parable about a shepherd, a flock, and a robber (vv. 1–5). It depicts a shepherd as one who has the right to access his flock through the door of the fold, in contrast to a thief, who has to clamber in by some other way.

The discourse that follows the parable is a kind of meditation on leading features of the parable. The mention of the door into the sheepfold is expanded in the passage beginning with "I am the Door of the sheep," while the reference to the shepherd of the sheep is developed in a description of the characteristics of the Good Shepherd. John Chrysostom observed, "When he brings us to the Father, he calls himself a *Door*, when he takes care of us, a *Shepherd*." The symbol of the Shepherd naturally is more comprehensive than that of the door, since it includes the thought of bringing people to God and caring for them, and thus leads to the thought of the Shepherd's laying down his life for the sheep.

The imagery of the Door has a notable precedent in Psalm 118:20: "This is the gate of the Lord, the righteous shall enter through it." In the saying of Jesus the picture of the Door is developed with respect to entrance into the salvation of the kingdom of God; in contrast to the "thieves and robbers," he has come in order that people may have "*life* . . . in its fullness" (John 10:8–10).

The *Good* Shepherd is so called in contrast to faithless shepherds and all who claim to be shepherds of humankind but are powerless to save. Over against them he is the one "genuine" Shepherd. The primary background to this contrast is the prophetic discourse in Ezekiel 34, where the displeasure of God with the "shepherds" of Israel, i.e., its rulers and leaders, is affirmed and where his intention to gather and care for the sheep himself is made known. So here, the emphasis on Jesus as the Good Shepherd underlines his genuine care for the sheep, which will issue in his laying down his life on their behalf (John

10:11). The imagery does not permit developing the thought in the direction of the Lord's laying down his life for the sins of the sheep(!), but it does enable the shepherd's knowledge of his sheep to be applied to a worthy goal for yielding his life on their behalf, as stated in vv. 14–15:

> I know mine and mine know me,
> as the Father knows me and I know the Father,
> and I lay down my life for the sheep.

The purpose of the Shepherd's death is here depicted under the image of sheep entering into a profound relationship with their "Shepherd"; on the human plane it portrays the kind of relationship that exists between the Father and the Son. We cannot help but recall the prayer of Jesus, that believers in the future may be one in the fellowship of the Father and Son, expressed in terms of mutual indwelling: "I in them and you in me, that they may be perfected in unity" (17:23).

(3) The link between 10:15 and 10:16 indicates that the death of Jesus is on behalf all nations: "I lay down my life for the sake of the sheep. And other sheep I have which do not belong to this fold, and those I must bring. . . ." Note, they are *his* sheep, even before they know anything about him, for they have been given to him by the Father (v. 29). Having given his life for them, the Shepherd of humanity intends to bring them into the one "fold," i.e., into the kingdom of God. Here is a hint that the mission of Jesus does not end with his death; *he* must gather his people!

The discourse is rounded off in vv. 17–18:

> For this reason my Father loves me, because I lay down my life, in order to take it again. Nobody takes it away from me, but I lay it down of my own accord. I have authority to lay it down, and I have authority to take it again. This command I received from my Father.

The imagery of shepherd and sheep has been left behind, but the thought is retained and expressed in plain speech. Two points are made. First, the Father's love for the Son is due to the Son's laying down his life for the world. Naturally the death of the Son is not to be interpreted as the *origin* of the Father's love, on the contrary, it is its greatest manifestation. The Father willed that the Son should lay down his life for humankind (v. 18), and the Son obeyed, in freedom and with sovereign authority from the Father. The mutual love of the Father and Son thus was seen in an act of love for the world, in which the Father in love willed to save all, and the Son in love freely gave himself for all. Second, Jesus lays down his life in order to take it up again. Here two thoughts come together: the unity of the death and resurrection of the Son for the salvation of the world and the attribution of the resurrection to the Son. Both characterize this Gospel and express an important understanding of the mission of the Son. The unity of the death and resurrection of Christ is expressed with particular clarity in the "lifting up" sayings of the Gospel, and we shall consider that feature in connection with them. The attribution of the resurrection to the Son is an outflow of the "sending" concept of the Gospel reflected in v. 18: "I have authority to lay down (my life), and I have authority to take it again. This command I received from my Father." The dying and the rising of the Son form the completion of the "works" given by the Father to the Son to do. The Son has more than once made it plain that he can do nothing of himself and that his works are really the works of the Father in him (so 14:10: "the Father abiding in me does his works," cf. also 5:19, 20). Accordingly, Schnackenburg had reason to affirm: "When, in rising from the dead, Jesus takes up his life again, nothing occurs other than that *the Father* glorifies him."[11]

In John 12:24–25 two isolated sentences have been incorporated into a group of sayings that relate to the death of Jesus:

> Amen, amen I tell you, unless a grain of wheat falls into the ground and dies, it remains alone; but if it dies it produces a great harvest. Anyone who loves his life loses it, and anyone who hates his life in this world will preserve it for eternal life.

These statements may be said to provide an exposition of the law of the kingdom of God: life is given through death. No explanation of the little parable about the grain of wheat is given, but its meaning is transparent: so surely as a grain of wheat must be buried if it is to yield fruit for the farmer, so the Son of Man must give himself in death if he is to produce a harvest of life for the world. It expresses in a pictorial manner a truth that we have seen stated in other sayings: the purpose of the death of Jesus is that humankind may enter into "life," but in this passage the necessity of the death of Jesus is emphasized.

In the sentence that follows, the "law" to which Jesus submits is applied generally: to love life is to lose it, to "hate" life is to keep it (in a context like this "hate" is a Hebraism for "love less," see Gen. 29:30–31; Luke 14:26 = Matt. 10:37). Observe, however, that the law of life through death in 12:24 has in view making life possible for *others*, whereas in v. 25 it is to gain life for *oneself.*

John 17:17–19 was viewed by B. F. Westcott as the focal point of the prayer of Jesus, and it led him to call the prayer, "The Prayer of Consecration." The passage reads:

> Consecrate them in the truth; your word is truth. As you sent me into the world I also sent them into the world; and for their sakes I consecrate myself, that they also may become consecrated in (the) truth.

Inevitably we recall the sayings of Jesus at the Last Supper, recorded in the first three Gospels and by Paul: "My body . . . on your behalf" (*hyper hymōn*, Luke 22:19); "My blood . . . on behalf of many" (*hyper pollōn*, Mark 14:24). These words, more clearly than any others in the synoptic Gospels, express the meaning of the death of Jesus; it is seen as a sacrifice by which a new covenant is initiated that humankind may inherit the kingdom of God. The petition of Jesus in John, "On their behalf I consecrate myself," has a similar significance. In the Old Testament the term "consecrate" in certain contexts can be synonymous with "sacrifice." In Deuteronomy 15:19, 21 we read:

> You shall *consecrate* to the Lord your God all the first-born males that are born of your herd and of your flock . . . But if it has any defect you shall not *sacrifice* it to the Lord your God.

There "consecrate" and "sacrifice" are plainly synonymous. That confirms what in any case should be the clear meaning of the prayer of Jesus: he consecrates himself *to death.* That he should consecrate himself in this manner reflects the consciousness of Jesus that he was sent by the Father for this purpose. His self-consecration to death brings his mission of mediating the saving sovereignty of God to its climax.

The last clause of John 17:19 should not go unnoticed: ". . . *for their sakes* (*hyper autōn*) I consecrate myself, *that they also may become consecrated in (the) truth.*" There is evidently an overlap in the meaning of the consecration of Jesus and that of his disciples. His dedication unto death is made in order that they may be dedicated to the task of bringing the saving sovereignty of God to the world *in a like spirit as he brought it.* Naturally he alone, through his unique obedience to death and exaltation to sovereignty, can introduce the saving kingdom into the world and open its doors for all; but his disciples can, and must, serve as its instruments as they proclaim the good news to the world and seek to embody it in their lives. This they will best do as they exemplify the suffering love of the Redeemer.

(4) A notable feature of the Fourth Gospel is its numerous references to the "hour" of Jesus. Mark has two occurrences of the word in relation to the sufferings of Jesus: 14:35, the prayer of Jesus in Gethsemane that the "hour" might pass from him, and 14:41, "The hour has come, the Son of Man is betrayed into the hands of sinners." Neither Matthew nor Luke has the Gethsemane reference, but both have the latter (or an equivalent). By contrast John has three occasions where the "hour" of Jesus is anticipated (2:4; 7:30; 8:20), and four which speak of the "hour" as having arrived (12:23, 27; 13:1; 17:1). We are constrained to ask, "The hour *for what*?" For his death, yes; but also for his exaltation and glorification. This latter feature in John's representation of the passion of Jesus has led not a few exegetes of recent times to affirm that the significance of the death of Jesus in the Fourth Gospel has quite changed. Bultmann asserted that in this Gospel the death of Jesus signifies two things: the completion of Jesus' obedience, and his release from his commission to return to the glory he formerly enjoyed.[12] Käsemann was emphatic about this notion: in his view the hour of the passion of Jesus is the hour of his glorification because *in it he leaves the world and returns to the Father;* the comprehensive word for the death of Jesus, therefore is *hypagein,* "to go away" (as in 13:1); in John's Gospel death for Jesus means separation from the world and return to the Father.[13] G. C. Nicholson is wholly persuaded by this view. He, too, seized on 13:1 as the key statement of the Gospel on this issue. According to it Jesus knew that his hour had come "that *he should pass over from this world to the Father,*" hence the hour of Jesus was the moment of his return to the Father. Naturally the crucifixion had a part in that hour, but it is not the primary element in it. If the "hour" in the synoptic Gospels signifies the death of Jesus (Mark 14:41), in John it is the moment of reunion with the Father.[14]

These theologians have obviously been profoundly impressed with the concept of the death of Jesus as his "glorification" or "exaltation"; but this combined with other factors which led them to a diminution of the significance of the death of Jesus in the Fourth Gospel which, I am convinced, the evangelist would have disowned.

Of the three anticipations of the "hour" of Jesus in the Gospel, two are related to a desire to arrest Jesus (7:30; 8:20), the first with the intention of seeking to put him to death (7:19–23, 25). The key saying as to the presence of the hour is not John 12:1 but 12:27:

> Now my heart is in turmoil. And what am I to say? "Father, save me from this hour." But for this purpose I came to this hour! "Father, glorify your name."

This passage is often called "the Johannine Gethsemane." Whether the evangelist has transferred the synoptic account of Jesus in Gethsemane to this point or is relating another occasion when Jesus so prayed, he undoubtedly has in view the same kind of shrinking from the death that lay ahead of him that Jesus experienced in Gethsemane. The verb used of the "turmoil" of Jesus signifies agitation, horror, convulsion, and shock of spirit—precisely the kind of thing that Mark described in his account of the agony in Gethsemane (Mark 14:34–41).[15] The utterance, "Father, save me from this hour," is best understood not as a question, but as the prayer which Jesus wanted to pray, and did pray, but could not go on praying. And why could he not? "For this cause I came to this hour." To endure that hour was the supreme purpose of his mission to humanity and the climax of the Father's commission to him. How then could he possibly retract from it? Accordingly Jesus prays that the Father will glorify his name.

It is impossible to reconcile this account of the agony of Jesus with the notion that in the Fourth Gospel the way to Golgotha was nothing but a victory parade and his death primarily a subsequent reunion with the Father. Jesus' continued sense of being in the will of his Father, and therefore of having authority from God in his hands, is unmistakable all through the Passion narrative; but the other side of that conviction is the cost of obedience on the part of the Son. John 12:27–28 provides a window into the struggle that it entailed for him.

Precisely these two elements, that the Father's will be performed and that the Son's obedience be carried through, are reflected in the last word of Jesus known to John, the cry uttered on the cross, "It is accomplished" (*tetelestai*). Observe, that utterance does not mean simply, "It is ended," but more strongly, "It is *achieved*," i.e., the purpose of his mission. Anton Dauer commented on this:

> So the last word of Jesus interprets his suffering and dying as the crowning conclusion and high point of the work that he has performed in obedience—the obedience of the Son finds here its most radical expression—and enables the believing eye to see the glorifying of the Son through the Father.[16]

(5) We now come to consider the most characteristic statements of the Fourth Evangelist on the death of Jesus, namely, those that speak of the "lifting up" of the Son of Man (3:14–15; 8:28; 12:32–34). Observe that while the first two sayings explicitly refer to the one who is lifted up as the Son of Man, the third has as subject a simple "I" ("I, if I be lifted up"); in 12:34, however, it is assumed by his hearers that Jesus spoke of the *Son of Man* as lifted up ("Who is this Son of Man?"), and the context is controlled by the utterance in v. 23, "The hour has come that the Son of Man be glorified." This is noteworthy, for these sayings remind us of the synoptic prophecies of the passion (especially John 3:14–15, "The Son of Man must be lifted up," compared with Mark 8:31, "The Son of Man must suffer much, . . . be killed, and after three days rise"). The startling difference between the two Gospel traditions is the condensation of the references to death and resurrection into a single term, *hypsothēnai*, "be lifted up." The rationale behind the synoptic predictions and the sayings in John is virtually the same: the event depicted in both groups is the eschatological action of the Son of Man in relation to the saving sovereignty of God. In the synoptics the death and resurrection of the Son of Man form the climax of his mediation of the kingdom of God in his ministry; in John the lifting up of Jesus forms the climax of his mission to bring life eternal to humankind.

The extent to which the use of the term "lifting up" in John has been determined by the linguistic background has been much debated. The old Aramaic *zeqaph* means to get up, lift up, hang up; it could signify, on the one hand, raising a criminal on a stake for his execution, and, on the other, lifting up one who is bowed down. In Ezra 6:11 it is used of impaling an offender, and in the Old Syriac (a form of Aramaic) and the Peshitta it translates in Mark 15:24 the term "crucify."[17] There are other Semitic terms, Hebrew and Aramaic, which have been suggested by scholars, with which we need not concern ourselves here.[18] One alternative suggestion, illustrating the word play involved in the idea of "lifting up," was put forward by David Daube (orally) in C. H. Dodd's New Testament seminar. In Genesis 40 Joseph interprets dreams of two fellow prisoners, a butler and a baker; to the former he says, "Within three days Pharaoh will *lift up* your head, and restore you to your office"; to the other he says, "Within three days Pharaoh will *lift up* your head—i.e., from you!—and hang you on a tree" (Gen. 40:19, cf. vv. 20–22, where the fulfillment is narrated). Dodd himself was impressed with this parallel and drew attention to it in his book on the Fourth Gospel.[19] H. Hollis, in a recent article on this issue, urged that this story fully explains the word play involved and that it would have been in the mind of Jesus when he used the term "lift up"; the link with the Joseph story, he believes, would have been recognized by his hearers.[20]

Along with the possible linguistic background must be reckoned a highly significant statement in the first stanza of the last Servant Song, Isaiah 52:13:

> My Servant will prosper (or be wise); he will be high, and lifted up, and greatly glorified.

This is rendered in the Septuagint:

> *Idou synesei ho pais mou kai hypsothēsetai kai doxasthēsetai sphodra . . .*

> My Servant will be wise
> and exalted and greatly glorified.

The passage is echoed in the hymn of Philippians 2:6ff.:

> Wherefore God *highly exalted* him,
> and gave him the name above every name . . .

It is extraordinary that both the terms "lift up" and "glorify" occur together in Isaiah 52:13 in relation to the sufferings and the death of the Servant of God; moreover, both occur in the Fourth Gospel in relation to the sufferings and death of the Son of God. There is a difference, however, between their applications, in the Servant Song and in the Gospel: the former has in view the exaltation of the Servant *after* his sufferings and death—observe that in Isaiah 53:10–12 the resurrection of the Servant is implied—whereas in John the lifting up and glorifying represent the death *and* the exaltation of Jesus as two inseparable stages of one event.

Before discussing these concepts further we should look at the texts. John 3:14–15 reads: "As Moses lifted up the snake in the desert, so the Son of Man must be lifted up, in order that everyone who believes may have in him eternal life." It is a kerygmatic statement, and it is fittingly followed by John 3:16. The way of salvation through the death of Jesus is illustrated by the incident of Moses lifting up a bronze replica of a snake for the healing of Israelites bitten by snakes (Num. 21:4–9). It is unrealistic to argue that the essential element here is the exaltation of the Son of Man to heaven rather than his crucifixion. The simple comparison is made of the lifting up of a "snake" on a pole that people in peril might live with the lifting up of the Son of Man on a cross that all who believe may have eternal life. Certainly both elements are in mind, the death on a cross and the exaltation to heaven, for it is "in him," in union with the living and exalted Savior, that life is received and experienced.

John 8:28 is a more ambiguous saying:

> When you lift up the Son of Man, then you will know that "I am (he)," and that I do nothing of my own accord, but speak only those things the Father has taught me.

No indication is given as to what is meant by the words, "When you lift up the Son of Man." The reader who knows the gospel of Christ crucified and risen will understand. Nor will the reader miss the point that it is "the Jews" who will "lift up" the Christ: i.e., *they* will bring about his death,[21] but it is *the Father* who will exalt him to heaven. An unusual feature of the saying is its presumption that the Jews responsible for the death of Jesus will afterwards come to know who he is, the nature of his ministry, and his relation to the Father. Is this an instance of knowing *too late*, as many think, or a prophecy of conversion? We cannot be sure: the possibility of both judgment and salvation may inhere in the saying.[22]

John 12:31–32 is fuller in content and of great significance for the Gospel:

Now is the judgment of this world, now the prince of the world will be thrown out, and I, if I am lifted up from the earth will draw all to myself.

The element of divine action is to the fore in this saying. "If I am lifted up" is a "divine passive"; it is God who exalts the Son of Man to his side. Both the context and the content of vv. 31–32 show that "if I am lifted up" denotes more than a simple return via death to the heavenly home of the Son of Man; in this event the judgment of the world takes place, the prince of this world is dethroned, and the Son of Man assumes the position of authority in the saving sovereignty under which all humanity may now come.

"The judgment of this world" is often interpreted in light of 3:19–21, i.e., as a process whereby humankind separates itself before the enthroned Son of Man, whether in faith or in unbelief. This is hardly plausible. In this context the judgment, like the "throwing out" of Satan and the "lifting up" of the Son of Man to the throne of God, appears to be an event. We are to understand it as the declaration of the decision of God with reference to humanity, characterized as it is by rebellion against God and readiness to follow "the prince of this world." So also the "rebellion" is not merely general, but concrete: the "now" of v. 31 refers to its expression in the rejection of the Son of Man and in putting him to death. Since the Son of Man is the representative of God, rejection of him as the One sent by him is rejection of the God who sent him. Therein sin is exposed in its most perverse form. Insofar as the judgment of the world is a revelation of its sin and occasion of its condemnation, the death on the cross is that moment. But it is more: in that event *God gave his Son that it might not perish in the judgment.* This is not reading into the saying something alien to it. Just as the first lifting up saying, 3:14–15, leads on to 3:16–17, so 12:31–32 follows sayings brought together by the evangelist which speak of the glorification of the Son of Man in a death for the world's salvation; the narrower and wider context of 12:31 in the Gospel demands that we interpret the judgment passed on "this world" as endured by the One whom "this world" murders. This turns the bad news of judgment for the rejection of the Son of

Man into the good news of deliverance through the lifting up of that same Son of Man. (The "wider context" in the Gospel includes the passages we have reviewed relating to the death of Jesus for the salvation of the world, namely, 1:29; 3:16–17; 6:51; 10:11–15, 17–18; 12:24–25; 17:17–19; 19:30.)

As an immediate consequence of this "lifting up," "the prince of this world" is "thrown out," i.e., from his place of authority. Apart from Luke 10:18, "I watched Satan fall, as lightning, out of heaven," the closest parallel to this statement is the "throwing out" of the "dragon" from heaven in Revelation 12. In the vision, an ancient story of a monster who sought to kill a woman's offspring that was destined to slay him, is used to depict the victory of Christ over the devil. The key to the Seer's use of the story is given in the utterance, "They overcame him on account of the blood of the Lamb"; it was through the death and exaltation of the Christ that the devil was overthrown. The picture is but one version of a myth known all over the ancient world that epitomized the defeat of the power of evil and that had become a kind of cartoon that could be freshly applied. No interpretation of the "throwing out" of Satan is offered in the Gospel; it is an image of defeat and judgment of the evil one and of the changed situation that has come about for humanity: through the exaltation of the Son of Man on the cross and to heaven, the devil is *dethroned* and the Christ *enthroned.*

The two statements on judgment are followed by a third that emphasizes the redemptive purpose of the death and exaltation of the Son of Man: "I, if I am lifted up from the earth, will draw all to myself." The lifting up of the Son of Man is not limited to a few feet above earth, but is to a position from where he can draw all to himself—to the throne of God in heaven. He draws all *to himself;* not to his cross, but to himself as the crucified-exalted Redeemer. Through his lifting up the saving sovereignty of God comes to the world, and the exalted Lord exercises his sovereignty as he draws all to him. The result is the same as in John 3:15: "that everyone who believes may have in him eternal life."

(6) A question arises: How does the *exaltation* of Jesus to heaven via his cross relate to the *glorifying* of Jesus through the Father and the glorifying of the Father through Jesus? As far as the former is concerned they virtually signify the same thing. We recall the prophecy about the servant in Isaiah 52:13: "He

will be wise, and be lifted up and greatly glorified." The cry of
Jesus in John 12:28 could have been programmed by that statement: "The hour has come that the Son of Man be glorified."
That the hour is one of suffering and death is seen in the immediately succeeding sentences: as a seed must die to bear fruit,
so the Son of Man must die to make the harvest of the kingdom
possible. But the prayer that the Father may glorify the Son in
that event (v. 28) is the burden of the Prayer of Consecration in
John 17. There it is a plea that the surrender of the life of Jesus
may be an acceptable sacrifice, that in it the Father may exalt
him to his presence in heaven and thus make his death and
exaltation the coming of the saving sovereignty through which
people may have eternal life (v. 2). The petition, then, in 12:28,
"Father, glorify your name," expresses the urgent desire of Jesus
that the Father may be glorified through his death. An answer
is given from heaven: "I have glorified it, and I shall glorify it
again." The Father has glorified his name through the ministry
of Jesus, and he is now to bring to a climax the revelation in the
submission of Jesus to death—itself a revelation of the Father's
love—and in his exaltation by the Father. The glorification, thus,
applies to the death-and-exaltation of Jesus—one indissoluble
event. And that is exactly what the "lifting up" of Jesus means.

All this comes together in 13:31–32. "Now the Son of Man
has been glorified": i.e., *God* has glorified him in making his
self-offering effective for the whole human race. "God has been
glorified in him": in that act God has been glorified through the
perfect obedience and love of the Son, which was also a revelation of God's love for all humanity. "If God has been glorified in
him (as he has!), God will glorify him in himself, and will glorify
him immediately"; i.e., God will glorify him in his own person,
and he will do that at once in the death and exaltation of Jesus.
We see therefore how "glorify" and "exalt" can coincide, even
though the concept of "glorify" can extend beyond exaltation.

(7) Having examined the relation between the exaltation
and the glory we must finally look at the relation between *the
exaltation and the resurrection* of Jesus. There is no mention of
our Lord's resurrection in the lifting up sayings. It is frequently
assumed that the death of Jesus was his exaltation by virtue of
its being his return to the Father, and the corollary is then drawn:
the resurrection can be of little or no theological significance
to John.[23] Yet such is not the impression made by the references

to the resurrection of Jesus in the Gospel. The riddlelike utterance of Jesus to the Jewish leaders: "Destroy this temple and in three days I will raise it" is interpreted by the evangelist as relating to the "temple of his body" (2:19–20). The "destruction" of the temple is likely to be viewed as a moral or spiritual degradation that destroys the nature of the temple as it was intended to be; it is further implied that continuance of the Jewish leaders in their way will end in the destruction of the body of Jesus, but that will be followed by a new spiritual temple, raised through the resurrection of Jesus and finding its locus in his risen body. That understanding of the new temple finds expression in the teaching on worship "in Spirit and in truth," which needs no material temple (4:21–24). Such teaching is revolutionary and can by no means be dismissed as of "little or no significance."

The same applies to the statement in 10:17–18:

> For this reason my Father loves me, because I lay down my life in order to take it again. . . . I have authority to lay it down and I have authority to take it again. This command I received from my Father.

There is no question of John's here taking up traditional language that does not fit his theology; it is completely Johannine and is set in the context of the mission of the Son, commissioned and authorized by the Father. The command to lay down his life and take it again is the supreme purpose of the mission, and the Son's obedient fulfillment of this commission is the reason for the Father's love toward him. That is central to the evangelist's theology.

The same must be said of the resurrection appearances of Jesus in the Fourth Gospel. They cannot justly be viewed as an appendage for which the evangelist has no theological use. The appearance to the disciples on Easter evening, narrated in chapter 20, is of particular importance. Never in all time has the common greeting of the Eastern world, "*Shalom* to you," borne such depth of meaning as when Jesus said it to his disciples that day. All that the prophets had poured into *shalom* as the epitome of the blessings of the kingdom of God had essentially been realized through the death and resurrection of Jesus for the world's salvation. It is the complement of his last utterance on the cross: "It is accomplished," for the peace and reconciliation and life of the Kingdom were now imparted to a group of men who received it and who were to make it known to the world.

The few sentences of Easter evening passed on by the evangelist convey a concentrated summary of the Easter revelation to the apostles and the commission given to them, which they were to share with the church. The appearance to Thomas has a special function. Only after the revelation of Easter can people make the confession that he made when confronted by the Risen Lord. So Paul indicates, when he cites the primitive confession: "If you confess *Jesus is Lord*, and believe in your heart that God raised him from the dead, you will be saved" (Rom. 10:9). Thomas declares the ultimate implication of the primitive confession. That people may make it their own is the purpose of the writing of our Gospel (20:30–31).

If, then, we have two theological convictions of importance to the evangelist, namely, resurrection and exaltation, we have no business dismissing one as of little account. It is rather the case that he will have seen no contradiction between the two. G. Bertram, in his article on *hypsoō* ("exalt") in the *Theological Dictionary of the New Testament*, affirmed the same thing. He maintained that there is no antithesis between exaltation and resurrection, though logically priority seems to belong to the former.

> Whether the New Testament references be to awakening, resurrection, reception, ascent, rapture, enthronement or royal dominion, all these can be summed up in the one word "exaltation."[24]

Now the evangelist himself gave a clear indication that he holds together the three concepts resurrection, glorification, exaltation. In recounting the cleansing of the temple and the enigmatic word of Jesus in 2:19, he wrote, "*When he was risen from the dead* his disciples remembered that he had said this"; but after describing the entry into Jerusalem he wrote, "*When Jesus was glorified* they remembered that these things were written about him. . . .*" From this Joseph Blank drew the conclusion, "It is thereby proved once for all that the glorification of Jesus includes his resurrection."[25]

Now that leads to a highly significant conclusion. Lifting up and glorification in relation to Jesus have in view the two moments of death and exaltation—glory on the cross and glory with God in heaven. Resurrection relates to him who died, was buried, and in whose transformed person was revealed the glory and exaltation that took place in the crucifixion and the exaltation with God. All three terms, accordingly, are needed to express the fullness of the redemptive event by which eternal life became the inheritance of all who respond in faith to the Son of God Redeemer. We cannot claim that this understanding of the Fourth Gospel has been or is now characteristic of the church's interpretation and proclamation of the gospel. But it is time that the greatness of the good news portrayed in the Gospel of John was freshly grasped and clearly proclaimed. It is the gospel of the incarnate Son of God, who revealed God in works given him by God to do and in words given him by God to say. His mission reached its momentous climax in an appalling death, through which the love of God in Christ was revealed; a death on a cross which pointed heavenward to the throne of God, to which he was going, and which in turn shed glory on him who reigned even on the cross. His horizontal cross-beam showed the worldwide extent of the redemption achieved for humankind; an event completed by his resurrection from the dead, which revealed the life eternal in which all who believe participate now, with the promise of an existence in the likeness of the Son of God in a new creation. In that event the mission of the Son of God reached its completion, only to continue without the limitations of flesh as he works on in the world and draws all to him in heaven. To receive in faith that ministry of the Son of God is to share his life. To make it known to the world is to share his joy.

NOTES TO 3

1. J. Denney, *The Death of Christ*, 1st edition 1902, revised edition without date, New York: G. H. Doran, pp. 181–82.

2. E. F. Scott, *The Fourth Gospel, Its Purpose and Theology*, Edinburgh: T. & T. Clark, 1906, p. 208.

3. Bultmann, *Theology of the New Testament*, vol. 2, p. 52.

4. Käsemann, *Testament of Jesus*, pp. 16–18.

5. G. Nicholson, *Death as Departure, The Johannine Descent-Ascent Schema*, SBLDS 63, Chico, California: Scholars Press, 1983, p. 143.

6. M. Meye Thompson, *The Humanity of Jesus in the Fourth Gospel*, Philadelphia: Fortress, 1989, p. 96.

7. "All on an April evening I heard the little lambs crying, and I thought on the Lamb of God."

8. It is not impossible that the source of John 19:31–37 had in view the Righteous Sufferer, while the evangelist, with his marked interest in the Exodus typology, had in view the Passover passages (so Bultmann, *Gospel of John*, 676–77; Barrett, *According to St. John*, p. 558; Schnackenburg (tentatively), *Gospel According to St. John*, vol. 3, p. 292. B. Lindars thinks that the evangelist had both typologies in mind, *The Gospel of John*, NCB, London: Oliphants, 1972, p. 590.

9. G. Vermes, "Baptism and Jewish Exegesis: New Light from Ancient Sources," *NTS* 4 (1958), p. 309. For the last citation, see *Exod. R.* 19.7. and *Melch. on Exod.* 12.6.

10. "If this event (of incarnation and death of Christ) is grounded in the love of God, it follows that God's love is the origin of the judgment. It is, of course, contrary to the intention of God's love, for he wishes not to judge, but to save the world (v. 17). Unbelief, by shutting the door on God's love, turns his love into judgment. For this is the meaning of judgment, that man shuts himself off from God's love." Bultmann, *Gospel of John*, p. 154.

11. Schnackenburg, *Gospel According to John*, vol. 2, p. 302.

12. Bultmann, *Theology of the New Testament*, vol. 2, pp. 52–53.

13. Käsemann, *Testament of Jesus*, pp. 18–19.

14. Nicholson, *Death as Departure*.

15. See the excellent discussion on this in W. Thüsing, *Die Erhöhung und Verherrlichung Jesu im Johannesevangelium*, 3d ed., Münster: Aschendorff, 1979, pp. 79–89.

16. A. Dauer, *Die Passionsgeschichte im Johannesevangelium, Eine traditionsgeschichtliche und theologische Untersuchung zu Joh 18:1–19, 30*, München: Kössel Verlag, 1972, p. 210.

17. See the illuminating article by G. Kittel, "*izdeqeph = hypsothē-nai = gekreuzigt werden*. Zur angeblichen antiochenischen Herkunft des vierten Evangelisten," *ZNW* 35 (1936), pp. 282–85. Many have been persuaded by Kittel's discussion, e.g., G. Bertram, "*hypsoō, ktl*," *TDNT*, vol. 8, p. 610, n. 38; M. Black, *An Aramaic Approach to the Gospels and Acts*, 2d ed., 1946; E. Schweizer, *Erniedrigung und Erhöhung*, 1955, p. 118; C. Colpe, "*hyios tou anthrōpou*," *TDNT*, vol. 8, p. 466; H. T. Wrege, "Jesusgeschichte und Jüngergeschick nach Joh 12:20–33 und Hebr 5:7–10: in *Der Ruf Jesu und die Antwort der Gemeinde, Festschrift J. Jeremias*, 1970, p. 271, n. 38; Barrett, *Gospel According to St. John*, p. 214.

18. Bertram draws attention to the use of *rum* in Ps. 9:13, "Thou who dost *lift me up* from the gates of death," rendered in the Septuagint, *ho hypson me ek ton pylon tou thanatou;* the same term appears in 1QH 6:34, 11:12 of raising from death for resurrection, while in Aramaic *'rim* means "take away" (*TDNT*, vol. 8, pp. 606–7). M. McNamara was attracted to C. C. Torrey's suggestion that the term *slq* used reflexively lay behind John 12:32; its reflexive form (*'stlq*) meant "be raised up," but more commonly "to go away, depart, die" (the same range of meanings is evident in the Hebrew use of the term; the reflexive Aramaic occurs in the Palestinian Targum to the Pentateuch in the sense of "die"; "The Ascension and the Exaltation of Christ in the Fourth Gospel," *Scripture* 19 [1967], pp. 66–69).

19. Dodd, *Interpretation,* p. 377.

20. H. Hollis, "The Root of the Johannine Pun—*hypsothēnai,*" *NTS* 35 (1989), pp. 475–78.

21. So Bultmann, *Gospel of John,* pp. 349–50; R. Brown, *Gospel According to John,* 2 vols., AB 29, 29A, Garden City: Doubleday, 1981, vol. 1, p. 351; C. K. Barrett (hesitatingly), *Gospel According to St. John,* p. 344; E. Haenchen, *Das Johannesevangelium,* ed. U. Busse, Tübingen: J.C.B. Mohr, 1980, p. 369, followed Bernard in thinking that the judgment of Jerusalem was in mind.

22. So R. Schnackenburg, *Gospel According to St. John,* vol. 2, pp. 202–3; J. Becker, *Evangelium des Johannes,* 2 vols., OTKNT 4/1,2, Gütersloh: G. Mohn, 1979, 1981, p. 296.

23. Such was Bultmann's belief: *Theology of the New Testament,* vol. 2, p. 56.

24. Bertram, *TDNT,* vol. 8, p. 611.

25. Blank, *Krisis,* p. 266, n. 5.

CHAPTER 4

THE MINISTRY OF THE HOLY SPIRIT

IT HAS OFTEN BEEN REMARKED that there are surprisingly few passages in the synoptic Gospels in which the Holy Spirit is mentioned, and of those, very few occur in sayings of Jesus. Mark speaks of the Holy Spirit five times, of which only three are in sayings of Jesus.[1] Matthew mentions the Holy Spirit twelve times; in them he reproduces Mark's three sayings of Jesus, plus one from Q, and the trinitarian formula for baptism in the missionary commission of the Risen Lord.[2] Luke has seventeen occurrences of the Holy Spirit, seven of which are in the birth narratives of chapters 1–2; he reproduces two of Mark's dominical sayings, plus the one Q saying which Matthew has; and he has three from his own tradition, one of which is in Isaiah 61:1, cited by Jesus in his Nazareth sermon.[3] By contrast John has twenty-five passages in which the Spirit is mentioned, fourteen of which are attributed to Jesus, plus the saying of the Risen Lord when he imparts the Holy Spirit.[4] Self-evidently there must be good reasons for this concentration of attention on the Holy Spirit by the Fourth Evangelist. We suggest some considerations that help to explain this feature of the Gospel.

(1) The Fourth Gospel was written with the conscious twofold perspective in mind of Jesus in his historical ministry to his own people, and Jesus the Risen Lord in his continuing ministry to the Jewish people and the nations of the world.[5] This is not entirely unique to John, inasmuch as each of the evangelists writes in the faith that Jesus, who labored for the kingdom of God in his earthly ministry, is now the Risen Lord at work in

the church and the world, and each evangelist directs his Gospel to the needs of the churches in his area; John exploits this understanding to the full. He emphasized the unity of the incarnate Lord in the flesh and in the resurrection era, and the continuity of his mission to the world through his disciples and his church. This necessitated the revelation to his followers of the ministry of the Holy Spirit, by whose power Jesus made God known in word and action in his ministry, and by whose inspiration his followers would make God known in their proclamation and continuation of his works. The presence of the Holy Spirit in the ministry of Jesus and as the representative of the Risen Lord in the church after Easter is the key to the history of Jesus in this Gospel.

(2) The supreme purpose in the mission of Jesus was to initiate the saving sovereignty of God. The redemption which the Son of God was sent to accomplish is an eschatological salvation, the prime element of which, as far as the individual is concerned, is life in the kingdom of God. It is evident in the Fourth Gospel that the inauguration of the saving sovereignty of God is a process coterminous with the work of Jesus, from the commencement of his ministry (see 1:51) to its climax in his death-resurrection-exaltation. It is in that final action that the kingdom fully comes; the Lord exercises his reign by drawing all to him (12:32) and by bestowing the life of the saving sovereignty on all believers. Now the evangelist shares the conviction of the Old Testament prophets, of contemporary Judaism, of Jesus, and of the writers of the New Testament that the Holy Spirit is *the Spirit of the kingdom of God*; he comes with the new age, when, as Joel put it, God "poured out" the Spirit on "all flesh" (2:28–32). So we read in John 7:39 the definitive statement, "The Holy Spirit was not yet given because Jesus was not yet glorified." That comment by the evangelist follows on the cry of Jesus in the Festival of Tabernacles,

> If any one is thirsty let him come to me, and let the one who believes on me drink. As the scripture said, "Rivers of living water will flow from his heart."

John interpreted the saying of the Spirit, whom believers were to receive, after the exaltation of the Lord to the position of authority in the saving sovereignty now fully come. In turn that assumes that the life eternal of the kingdom of God is mediated by the Holy Spirit. Since life through Christ is the key concept of salvation, it is evident that the sending of the Spirit is of crucial importance in the thought of the evangelist.

(3) The mission of Jesus is not only to redeem, but to reveal God to humankind. This he accomplished through his teaching and his works (his *signs*), which culminated in his death and resurrection and which constituted the supreme revelation of God. The comprehension of this revelation required the ministry of the Holy Spirit, a feature strongly emphasized in the discourses of Jesus in the Upper Room. One of the outstanding elements of the Fourth Gospel is the constant misunderstanding of Jesus by his hearers, both his disciples and his opponents (cf. 2:19–22; 3:3–4; 4:13–15, 31–34; 6:41–42 etc.). Toward the close of the Upper Room discourses Jesus acknowledges, "I have been speaking to you in the obscure speech of metaphor" (16:25). That saying could extend beyond the context to which it refers to the whole instruction of Jesus in the Gospel. It is, however, followed by the affirmation:

> A time is coming when I shall no longer use obscure language to you but shall speak to you openly about the Father.

Since Jesus is about to die, that instruction of his "in plain speech" is clearly to take place through the Holy Spirit. And that ministry of revelation through the Spirit is the predominant theme of the work of the Paraclete-Spirit described in John chapters 14–16.

(4) An important element of the context of the ministry of the Spirit in our Gospel is linked with the representation of the ministry of Jesus as a great *trial.* J. Blank wrote:

> The motif of a trial runs through the entire gospel like a scarlet thread.[6]

The "trial" is concerned with determining who is in the right, Jesus or the world as represented by the Jews. The background of this mode of presenting the conflict between Jesus and his people is the "lawsuit" of God with Israel and the nations, depicted in Deutero-Isaiah, especially in Isaiah 43:8–13, 25–28, and 44:6–11. The evangelist sees Israel faced with the question whether it will recognize in the claim of Jesus the claim of God. On this F. Porsch commented:

> In the decision against Jesus, the One sent by God, the relationship
> to God himself is decided, and with the eschatological salvation.[7]

To this end witnesses who attest the validity of the claims of
Jesus are cited, notably in John 5:31–47; there the witness of
God is adduced that he gave through John the Baptist, the works
of Jesus, the scriptures, and Moses. Self-evidently the disciples
of Jesus, and the church which springs from their ministry, are
also called to bear witness to Jesus. Their situation is rendered
the more difficult in that the "trial" of Jesus continues after his
death in the world's opposition to and arraignment of those
who believe in him. This opposition of the world to the church
is most vividly set forth in John 15:18–16:4, where the hatred of
the world against Jesus is represented as directed against his
followers:

> Indeed, the hour is coming when anyone who kills you will sup-
> pose that he is offering a service to God.

In that circumstance the great witness to Jesus will come to
the disciples' aid, namely, the Holy Spirit, to whom the name
"Paraclete" is given. That is the burden of the promises relating
to the sending of the Spirit in the Upper Room discourses. The
situation of the church after Easter is in mind. The world has
condemned and put to death God's representative, but God has
vindicated him through resurrection and exaltation to lordship
of his saving sovereignty. As the church bears witness to Jesus
as Lord, the Holy Spirit joins in witness with them and makes
that witness effective (15:26–27). So he opens people's eyes to
see that the Jesus who was condemned and executed by the
world was really in the right; it is accordingly the world that is
on trial, and Jesus is now the judge. F. Porsch has expressed this
aspect of the ministry of the Spirit thus:

> He is the chief witness of Jesus, but not in a spectacular "show trial"
> before the world . . . but in that invisible trial that takes place in the
> conscience of every individual who is confronted with the claim of
> Jesus. John accordingly has undertaken a transposition out of the
> public legal sphere into the interior of a person. *There* the trial now
> takes place, *there* the Paraclete bears witness for Christ, *there* is the
> place of judgment.[8]

Thus the mission of the church is carried out by the aid of
the Holy Spirit. He is furthermore the key to the church's un-

derstanding of the revelation brought through Jesus and of the witness which the church must bear to Jesus before the world.

Below it will be our task to review the passages in which the evangelist has set forth the ministry of the Holy Spirit in the Gospel. We will pay particular attention to (1) the witness of John the Baptist; (2) the authority of the revelation through Jesus; (3) baptism and the Holy Spirit; (4) the Holy Spirit and the Lord's Supper; (5) the Spirit of the Living Water; (6) the assurance of eternal life; (7) the Holy Spirit and worship; (8) the Holy Spirit as Paraclete (John 14–16); and (9) the mission of the Spirit and the mission of the church.

(1) John 1:29–34: *The Witness of John the Baptist*

It is clear that the witness of John to Jesus in the paragraph before us centers on the baptism of Jesus by John. Why the evangelist does not mention the event explicitly is beyond our knowledge. He knew well that every Christian reader of his Gospel would recognize the occasion, and he had no wish to dissociate Jesus from baptism as a rite, as is indicated by his account of the extraordinarily successful baptizing ministry of Jesus in Judea, contemporaneous with John's ministry (3:26–27; 4:1–3). It is at least plain that the evangelist viewed the descent of the Spirit on Jesus as the most important element in the baptism of Jesus. One unexpected aspect of the Spirit's descent on Jesus is stressed by the evangelist, namely, the revelation of Jesus' identity thereby made and the purpose of John's baptism. When the Pharisees asked why John was baptizing if he was not the Messiah, or Elijah, or the prophet, the reply was given: "There is one standing in your midst whom you do not know" (1:26); the continuation of this sentence in v. 31 shows he was referring to the Messiah. This reflects the contemporary view of the hidden Messiah: he would be born of David's line and would grow up without him or anyone else knowing who he was destined to be; then the time would come when he would be revealed—a popular belief was that he would be anointed by Elijah.[9] John 1:26 is completed in v. 31:

> I did not know who he was, but I came baptizing in water for the purpose of his being revealed in Israel.

The revelation was made when the Spirit descended as a dove from heaven, and it *remained on him* (v. 32). Without doubt we are to recall the prophetic utterances of Isaiah 11:1–2 and 42:1, which declare that the Spirit of the Lord will *rest* on the Messiah (elaborated in 11:1–2), and that by virtue of the Lord's bestowing his Spirit on him he will fulfill his messianic task of bringing justice to the nations (42:1–4). The Baptist's way of stating that messianic task is expressed differently:

> He who sent me to baptize in water said to me, "You will see the Spirit coming down and remaining on someone; *this is the one who is to baptize in Holy Spirit*" (John 1:33).

The same testimony of John concerning the Messiah is given by the synoptists. Mark has the same language ("he will baptize in Holy Spirit"), but Matthew and Luke record the Q testimony, "he will baptize in Spirit and fire" (Matt. 3:11; Luke 3:16). Clearly the Messiah's baptism, according to the Q, stresses the element of judgment through the agency of the mighty Spirit (cf. Isa. 4:4; Mal. 3:1–6; 4:1–2), but not exclusively so: the Messiah is to baptize *all* with Spirit and fire; for God's people it will mean refinement and renewal for the kingdom of God (as in Mal. 3:1ff.); for the reprobate it will be with consuming power (as in Mal. 4:1). In the Johannine narrative the positive result in renewal for the life of the kingdom of God is presumably alone in view.

The result of this revelation concerning Jesus and the Spirit is made known in John 1:34: "I have seen it, and borne witness that this man is the Son of God." For which cause the whole episode is enclosed in the testimony of 1:29 and 36: "Look, the Lamb of God! (the One who takes away the sin of the world"; v. 29). The church, the Jews, the whole wide world are called upon to listen to the witness of the last of the prophets to the man on whom the Spirit abides.

(2) John 3:34: *The Authority of the Revelation through Jesus*

The theme of the paragraph in which v. 34 is set is the supremacy of the revelation of him who comes "from above," i.e., from the Father, and who bears witness to "what he has seen and heard" (v. 32). The language appears to include reminiscence of a pre-incarnate existence with the Father. Passages such as 5:19–20, 30, however, speak of a constant fellowship between the Father and the Son as the source of his words and works; the continuing fellowship of the Father and Son, prior to incarnation, during the earthly life, and in the post-resurrection era is a foundational christological assumption in the Gospel.

The evangelist continues in his meditation by affirming, "whoever has accepted his witness has set his seal to the fact that God is true" (3:33); i.e., he has authenticated the truthfulness of God, since the Son bears witness to what God has given him to say. This the Son can do because "he does not give the Spirit in a limited measure (to him)." The dictum of Rabbi Aha is often cited to illustrate this saying: "The Holy Spirit who rests on the prophets rests on them only by measure."[10] To the Jews the Holy Spirit is especially the Spirit of prophecy. The immeasurable gift of the Spirit to the Son suggests perfection of revelation through him. While it is possible grammatically to view "the one whom God sent" as the subject of *didōsin* ("gives"), and thus to see the Son as the giver of the Spirit, the content demands that the Son is here the *receiver* of the Spirit "without measure." This is confirmed in the sentence that follows v. 34: the Father "has placed all things into his hand," i.e., he has bestowed on him authority in both revelatory utterance and action. As G. M. Burge rightly observes:

> John 3:34 links three important Johannine themes: Jesus' mission (*apostellō*, "send"), Jesus' revelation (*laleō, martyreō*, "speak," "witness"), Jesus' anointing (*to pneuma ouk ek metrou*, "the Spirit without measure"). Jesus has been sent by God to reveal the very Father whose gift of the Spirit ascertains his revelation.[11]

(3) John 3:5: *Baptism and the Holy Spirit*

The subject of sacraments in the Fourth Gospel is to be given fuller consideration later. Here we must be content with briefer treatment.

The explosive statement of v. 3 (as Nicodemus will have viewed it), "Unless one is begotten from above he cannot see the kingdom of God," is explained in v. 5. "Unless one is begotten of water and Spirit he cannot enter the kingdom of God." To be begotten "from above," i.e., from God, is defined as being begotten "by water and Spirit." That is most naturally understood of baptism in water and the Messiah's baptism in Spirit. There is some hesitation among scholars to accept this interpretation. G. M. Burge unhesitatingly affirms it, but he modifies it. He rightly comments on the phrase "of water and Spirit":

> Since both nouns are anarthrous and are governed by a single preposition, what we most likely have is a hendiadys in which both terms should be coordinated to give a single concept. This means

that 3:5 reflects the typical Johannine idiom of "pairs in tension." The significance of the one spills over into the other; and as often is the case, the accent falls on the second noun.[12]

That is surely right. The emphasis falls on the Spirit's work. But Burge deduces from vv. 6–8:

The contributing features of the "water" are now dismissed; in its synthesis with Spirit, its role has been rendered superfluous.[13]

That deduction is without warrant. One should recall that the Fourth Evangelist, alone among the Gospel writers, draws attention in this very chapter to the fact that the Messiah as well as the forerunner was authorizing a baptism in water, and that the populace was flocking in larger numbers to the Messiah's baptism than to John's (3:26; 4:1–2). One who presents the Nicodemus discourse alongside this comparison is hardly wishing to dismiss the role of baptism as "superfluous." On the contrary, Nicodemus is reminded that he, as all others, should respond to the call to repentance proclaimed by John and Jesus and expressed in baptism, for he also needs cleansing and renewal by the Spirit if he is to enter the kingdom of God. In the context of the conversation, the two gifts of God are separated as present bestowal and eschatological hope, for the Messiah's baptism in the Spirit awaits his death and exaltation to heaven, whence he will send the Spirit (7:39; 20:22). In the time of the church, however, baptism in water and baptism in Spirit are to become a unified experience for one who repents and believes in the crucified and risen Savior (3:14–16).

The radical nature of the birth from above is emphasized in the contrast of flesh and Spirit, v. 6: "What is begotten of flesh is flesh, and what is begotten of Spirit is spirit." "Flesh" in the Bible typically speaks of the weakness of human beings as creatures (see especially Isa. 31:3: "The Egyptians are men, not God; their horses are flesh, not Spirit"); by contrast the Spirit is the power of God at work in the world. The parabolic saying in John 3:8 exemplifies the reality but also incomprehensibility of the work of the Spirit in humankind:

The wind blows where it wills, and you hear its sound, but you do not know where it is coming from and where it is going to; so it is with everyone who is begotten of the Spirit.

There is, of course, a play on the word "wind" (*pneuma*) here, for it is the basic term for "spirit." Alike in Hebrew, Aramaic, and Greek, the double meaning in the term wind/Spirit is evident; and so is the lesson: "What those who have been born of the Spirit are, whence they come and whither they go, is incomprehensible to the world; as incomprehensible as Jesus himself is to the Jews."[14]

(4) John 6:63: *The Holy Spirit and the Lord's Supper*

It is perhaps surprising that no mention is made of the Holy Spirit in the discourse on the Bread of Life. The perceptive reader of the Gospel will know that the Spirit's work is presumed in all that is said of the gift of life through the Son. But the net result of the discourse among many of Jesus' disciples is offense at its teaching. They stumbled at its insistence on the real incarnation of the Son of God in Jesus—his "descent" from heaven—and at its emphatic imagery of eating his flesh and drinking his blood to share in his redemption. The response of Jesus to this offense is to point to the occasion when they will have real cause to be offended, namely, when they see him "ascending" where he was before *through his death on a cross*. Then they really will be shocked! But that saying points to the intent of the discourse: the life of the kingdom of God for which the Jews look is given through the death and resurrection of Jesus. That is when "eating" and "drinking" his flesh and blood will be possible. And that is the heart of v. 63, which is commonly acknowledged to be the key to the discourse on the Bread of Life:

> It is the Spirit who gives life, the flesh counts for nothing; the words that I have spoken to you are Spirit and life.

Flesh as such, whether given or eaten, cannot produce God's salvation. But the Son of God given in sacrifice for the life of the world, raised and exalted to the right hand of the Father, will send his Spirit so that men and women may be united with him in his sacrificial self-giving, and so participate in the life of the saving sovereignty. This is how people may receive the Christ and obtain life in him; and they continue to receive as they eat and drink his flesh and blood in the daily walk of faith, but most especially in the fellowship of the Lord's Supper. The words of Jesus, accordingly, are "Spirit and life," since those who receive them and believe in the Son receive the Spirit and the life of which he speaks (as in 5:39–40 and 7:37–39).

The nature of this life in Christ by the Spirit is the theme of the discourses spoken in the context of the Last Supper, chapters 13–17.

(5) John 7:37–39: *The Spirit and Living Water*

If anyone is thirsty let him come to me, and let him drink who believes in me.

As the scripture said, "Rivers of living water will flow from his heart."

Now this he said about the Spirit, which they who believed in him were to receive, for the Spirit was not yet (given) because Jesus was not yet glorified.

This saying of Jesus at the Festival of Tabernacles has in view the water given by God during the time of the Exodus and that expected in the second Exodus; i.e., the water that sprang from the rock for the thirsty Israelites in the wilderness (Exod. 17:1–6) and the river of living water to flow from the temple in Jerusalem in the kingdom of God (Ezek. 47:1–11; cf. also Zech. 14:8). The word of Jesus implies that as God intervened to save his people in the past and promised fullness of blessing in the coming kingdom, so Jesus offers that gift of water in the present. What gift is that? Jews interpreted gift of water in varied ways. In the Old Testament it is applied to God himself, "the fountain of living waters" (Jer. 17:13; see Zech. 14:8); in Judaism to the law ("As water is life for the world, so are the words of the Tora life for the world," Sifra Deut. 11,22) and to Wisdom ("Those who eat me will hunger for more, and those who drink me will thirst for more," Ben Sira 24:21), and not infrequently to the Holy Spirit. Among rabbinical sayings illustrating this last application there are several which specifically link the water-drawing ceremony of the Feast of Tabernacles with the Holy Spirit, e.g., b. Sukkah 5:55a:

Why did they call it (the court of the women) the place of drawing water? Because it was from there that they drew the Holy Spirit, according to the word, "with joy you will draw water out of the wells of salvation."

So, too, the evangelist in 7:39 interpreted the utterance of Jesus as relating to the Holy Spirit sent from the crucified, risen, and exalted Lord. The saving sovereignty having decisively come through that event, the exalted Lord releases him for the disciples, and so for the world (20:22–23); and consequently the Spirit's ministry in the world is directed to communicating the life of the kingdom of God to humankind, as indicated in John 3:3, 5, 6–8.

(6) John 4:13–14: *The Assurance of Eternal Life*

The foregoing passage from the Festival of Tabernacles makes clear the meaning of the statement of Jesus to the Samaritan woman at Jacob's Well:

> Everyone who drinks this water will become thirsty again, but whoever drinks the water that I shall give him will never become thirsty any more, but the water that I shall give him will become a fountain of water in him, perpetually flowing for eternal life.

As in the former saying, "the gift of God" which Jesus has come to bestow on people (v. 10) denotes the life mediated by the Spirit, who is to be sent from the crucified and exalted Redeemer. The difference between the two sayings is that the former is represented as water from a boundless stream, and the latter is depicted as an inexhaustible well within the believer, fed by a constantly flowing fountain. The water is not depicted as given to pass on to others; it is rather an assurance of life for the believer from the Spirit who ever remains to bind him to the Lord of life.

(7) John 4:23–24: *The Holy Spirit and Worship*

> The hour is coming and it is here already, when the genuine worshippers will worship the Father in the Spirit and in the truth; for the Father is seeking just such people to worship him. God is Spirit, and those who worship him must worship in the Spirit and in the truth.

In the conversation of Jesus with the Samaritan woman beside Jacob's well, he had virtually reached the point where he had told the woman "all that she had ever done" (cf. 4:29). She in response raised the most burning issue between Samaritans and Jews: where God should be worshipped, whether in Jerusalem or at the place where God had commanded that worship be offered him after the Jews arrived in the promised land; in the Samaritan version of the law that was Mount Gerizim.[15] Jesus dismisses the argument. The hour is coming—and it is already present—when God will manifest his presence, i.e., in the kingdom he has promised, when he will be known and loved and adored as never before (cf. Rev. 21:3–4). In this Gospel, however, the "hour" denotes especially the hour of the death and glory of Jesus (cf. 12:23; 13:1; 17:1), when the saving sovereignty of the future, already in the process of coming through the word and works of Jesus, moves to its ordained climax. Then the Spirit will be released for a new kind of worship that will not be tied down to the temple of Jerusalem or to the ruins of Gerizim's temple, but people will be freed for fellowship with the Risen Lord, who is himself the temple of the new age (John 2:17–19). *That* will be worship "in the Spirit and in the truth." Notice that the expression does not mean in a "spiritual" and sincere manner or, as C. H. Dodd understood it, with the mind, and as dealing with ultimate reality.[16] Rather, it is to be interpreted as *in virtue of the life, freedom, and power of the Spirit,* and *in accordance with the redemptive revelation brought by the Redeemer,* whose name and nature is truth (14:6).

This declaration is rooted in the way God has revealed himself and accomplished his redeeming works. "God is Spirit" defines God, not in his metaphysical being, but according to his work in the world. The clause is parallel in this respect to "God is light" (1 John 1:5), and "God is love" (1 John 4:8). On this Schlatter commented: "All these statements describe *God's mode of action and working.*"[17] So also Bultmann wrote:

> The *pneuma* (Spirit) is God's miraculous dealing with man which takes place in the revelation. . . . "God is Spirit" defines the idea of God by saying what God *means,* namely that for man God is the miraculous being who deals wonderfully with him, just as the definition of God as *love* refers to him as the one who deals with men out of his love and in his love.[18]

When therefore a person believes in Jesus and opens heart and mind to him, the Holy Spirit enables such a one to give exactly that kind of worship the Father seeks from all people.

(8) John 14–16: *The Holy Spirit as Paraclete*

The most characteristic teaching on the Holy Spirit in John's Gospel is contained in five sayings in the Upper Room discourses which speak of the Spirit as the Paraclete (14:15–17, 25–26; 15:26–27; 16:7–11, 12–15). H. Windisch held that these sayings are small units that can be removed from their contexts without leaving gaps—in fact their omission *improves* the context! He urged that the evangelist took over these sayings, applied them to the Spirit in the church, and focused the Spirit's witness on Jesus. In so doing he presented the Spirit-Paraclete as having three tasks, namely, as (a) a witness who vindicates and judges (15:26; 16:8–14); (b) a helper and an aid (14:16–17); (c) a counselor and teacher (14:26; 16:12–15).[19] Many scholars have been persuaded by Windisch's arguments, while taking exception to some of his ideas, above all the notion that the Paraclete sayings are *alien* to the discourses; on the contrary, there are those who think that the passages so well harmonize with their contexts that it is difficult to envisage that they ever existed apart from their present position. In my judgment the Paraclete sayings do form a coherent body of utterances about the Holy Spirit. They show a clear progression of thought, but the central one, 15:26–27, provides the key to the rest. It is closely parallel to a saying found in Mark 13:11 and the Q passage, Matthew 10:19–20/Luke 12:11–12; it assures the disciples of the Holy Spirit's aid when they are placed on trial, presumably by reason of their preaching the gospel of Christ. Interestingly, the contexts of the saying in the three synoptic Gospels are all different, and that in John's Gospel is different again, indicating that the saying circulated in the early churches as an independent logion. The feature common to Matthew, Mark, and John is the continuation by the disciples of the mission of Jesus in the face of the opposition of the world. It is likely that the other Paraclete sayings clustered around this one, for they are related to it thematically, and furthermore it gives us the clue to the use of the word Paraclete.

The term *Paraclete* comes to us straight from the Greek language and means "one called alongside." It was commonly used of one called to help in a court case, but it never became a recognized technical term (unlike the Latin *advocatus*, similar in form, but meaning a professional legal representative; compare our modern terms lawyer, attorney, barrister). Nevertheless J. Behm summarized the linguistic use as follows:

> The history of the term in the whole sphere of known Greek and Hellenistic usage outside the New Testament yields the clear picture of a legal adviser or helper or advocate in the relevant court. (The passive form does not rule out the idea of the *paraklētos* as an active speaker "on behalf of someone before someone," nor is there any need of recourse to the active of *parakaleō* [to call] in this connection.)[20]

Now this raises a problem: the term Paraclete brings to mind an individual called to aid another in a trial: such a meaning is eminently suitable to John 15:26–27 and 16:8–11; the former indicates a barrister for the defense, the latter one who accuses or brings charges against defendants. Yet in the other sayings the Paraclete has quite different functions: in 14:16–17 and 16:7 he has the role of one who takes the place of Jesus to aid his disciples, and in 14:26 and 16:12–15 his task is specifically to reveal the truth set forth in the life and teaching of Jesus. How do we reconcile this usage of the term Paraclete with his function regarding revelation? The answer appears to lie in the presentation of Jesus as involved in the greatest trial of history. We have referred to this motif already, as it appears in the narrative of the ministry of Jesus, but it is of central significance also in the discourses of chapters 14–16. Jesus is depicted as opposed and condemned by this world, and his disciples are set in a similar situation through their relation to him. It is in this context that the Paraclete is to be sent to the disciples of Jesus, to *bear witness to him* and to his word and work. This he will do directly *in* the disciples, but also *with* them and *through* them. Accordingly, another name is given to him in this ministry, "the spirit of Truth" (14:17; 15:26; 16:13). It is of no small interest that this term was current in contemporary Judaism, notably in the Qumran community. Also, in the Testament of Judah 20:1–5 we read this significant passage:

> Understand, my children, that two spirits await an opportunity with humanity: the spirit of truth and the spirit of error. In between is the conscience of the mind which inclines as it will. The things of truth and the things of error are written in the affections of man, each one of whom the Lord knows. There is no moment in which man's works can be concealed, because they are written on the heart in the Lord's sight. And the spirit of truth testifies to all things and brings all accusations. He who has sinned is consumed in his heart and cannot raise his head to face the judge.[21]

There is a comparable description of the "spirit of truth" and a "spirit of perversity" in 1QS 3:18–21, where they are named the Prince of Light and the Angel of Darkness. Such citations illustrate not the dependence of John on such writings but the familiarity of these ideas in contemporary Judaism. The Paraclete-Spirit in John has the unique task of bearing witness to the truth *which is in Jesus* (14:6).

Finally we should note that the first mention of the Paraclete in John speaks of him as *"another* Paraclete" (14:16), with the clear implication that Jesus is also a Paraclete. Inevitably we recall 1 John 2:1, the only passage outside John 14–16 where the term occurs:

> If anyone sins we have a Paraclete with the Father, Jesus Christ, the Righteous One.

Here Jesus is depicted as an intercessor *in* the court of heaven, representing the cause of his own, whereas the Holy Spirit is the Paraclete *from* heaven, supporting his own in the face of a hostile world. The ministries of the two Paracletes, however, are thought of not as *simultaneous*, but as successive. The Spirit-Paraclete takes the place of the Paraclete Jesus after Jesus' departure to the Father.

We shall now briefly review the presentation of the ministry of the Spirit-Paraclete in John 14–16.

John 14:16–17

> I shall ask the Father, and he will give you another Paraclete that he may be with you forever. The Spirit of Truth, whom the world cannot receive, because it does not know him, but you are to know him, because he will dwell with you and will be in you.

The fact that the "other Paraclete" is to be with the disciples "forever" confirms the generally accepted understanding that he is to be *the successor* to Jesus and is to remain with them "unto the age," i.e., till the revelation of the kingdom of God. The continuity of the work of the two Paracletes is clear, as also is the parallelism between their functions, specifically in relation to the one work of establishing the saving sovereignty of God in the world. It is conceivable that the roles of Jesus and the Holy Spirit in relation to the "trial" of the Lord and his disciples are also in view; in that case Jesus as the exalted Lord is now the judge, and the Spirit-Paraclete takes on his task of accusing the world and defending the followers of Jesus.[22]

It is noted that the "world" cannot receive or see or know the Spirit. As Bultmann remarked:

> The world *qua* world cannot receive the Spirit; to do so it would have to *give* up its essential nature, that which makes it the world.[23]

This incapacity to receive the revelation and enter into communion with the Spirit is due to the world's rejection of the revelation in Jesus and consequent blindness under the judgment of God. To bring this home to those who belong to the world is part of the Paraclete's task (16:8–11). By contrast the disciples will come to know the Paraclete because "he will remain alongside you and will be in you." That is, his presence will be known among them and within them.

John 14:25–26

> I have spoken these things to you while remaining with you; but the Paraclete, the Holy Spirit, whom the Father will send in my name, will teach you everything, and will remind you of everything that I have said to you.

The opening clause appears to relate not only to the teaching of Jesus in the discourse prior to this point, but to his "word" generally, as in vv. 23–24. Jesus is near the completion of his ministry; he is about to depart this life, and the Paraclete is shortly to assume his task. Observe that the Paraclete is to be sent by the Father "in the name of" Jesus. Jesus was sent in the name of his Father (5:43), i.e., as his representative; the Paraclete is sent in the name of Jesus and is thus *his* representative. His task is to *teach* the disciples everything and *remind* them of everything, i.e., of what Jesus said. The two tasks are complementary, almost identical; the Spirit will enable the disciples to *recall* the teaching of Jesus and to *understand* its meaning; by those means the disciples will come to grasp the revelation of God in Christ in its richness and profundity.

Two lessons seem clear from this saying: first, the Spirit brings no new revelation—he reminds disciples of the teaching of Jesus and enables them to comprehend it; second, the role of the Spirit as representative of Jesus and his task of recalling and interpreting the revelation brought by him show the personal nature of the Spirit. The trinitarian implications of the doctrine of the Paraclete are already evident.

John 15:26–27

> When the Paraclete comes, whom I shall send to you from the Father, the Spirit of Truth who comes forth from the Father, he will bear witness, because you have been with me from the beginning.

The Spirit's task is here set forth as "bearing witness" to Jesus. In this context Porsch thought that that meant his acting as a *prosecuting* attorney or as one giving evidence *against* the world. He was encouraged in this understanding in light of the similar statement in Mark 13:9–11:

> You will be handed over to local councils and flogged in the synagogues. On account of me you will stand before governors and kings as witnesses to them. And the Gospel must first be preached to all nations. Whenever you are arrested and brought to trial, do not worry beforehand what to say. Just say whatever is given you in that hour, for it is not you speaking but the Holy Spirit.

Porsch assumed that this Markan passage depicts at one and the same time speech of defense (of the disciples) and accusation (of the court), and therefore the same applies to the Johannine passage; it is directed *against* the world in its opposition to the gospel.[24] Admittedly there are interpreters of Mark 13:9–11 who come up with this view, but it appears to me transparently clear that Mark is describing occasions when the Spirit will enable disciples, in making their defense, to bear a powerful witness to their opponents and judges. We recall sermons recorded in the book of Acts, where apostles set in circumstances of hostility and in judicial courts use the occasions to preach the gospel (cf. Acts chapters 7, 22, 23, 26). For this reason Mark places at this point a declaration of Jesus that "the gospel must be preached to all nations"; he sees that this is precisely the kind of context in which the gospel is to go forth to all the world. (Luke's paraphrase of the Lord's directive in Luke 21:13–15 brings out this aspect of mission in the courtroom even more distinctly: "You will be arrested and persecuted . . . tried in synagogues . . . brought before kings and rulers. . . . This will be your chance to tell the Good News" [GNB]). It is evident that John 15:26–27 should be interpreted in the light of the familiar trial imagery of the Gospel wherein the disciples are depicted as arraigned before the world's tribunal; their defense is primarily to witness to Jesus, with intent not only to secure acquittal but still more to win over their opponents and judges. As they do this the Spirit-Paraclete will at the same time bear his witness in the minds and hearts of the hearers.

John 16:7–11

> I am telling you the truth; it is to your advantage that I am going away. For if I do not go away the Paraclete will not come to you; but if I go away I will send him to you. And he, when he comes, will

> expose the world with respect to sin, and righteousness, and judgment; with respect to sin, in that they are not believing in me; with respect to righteousness, inasmuch as I am going away to the Father, and you will no longer see me; with respect to judgment, inasmuch as the prince of this world has been judged.

The statement that Jesus must depart before the Paraclete can come has led to some questionable exegesis. It is viewed as affirming "the impossibility of a concurrent ministry of the two Paracletes" and implying that "so long as the dominant personality of their Master was at their side the disciples could not grow to their full stature."[25] Neither assertion is justifiable. Nor is the asseveration of Porsch, that the future presence of the Paraclete is better than the bodily presence of Jesus. What Porsch apparently had in mind is more carefully expressed in his statement:

> Only after Jesus' departure to the Father can the Paraclete demonstrate who he really is. To that extent full faith was possible only after the completion of the work of Jesus.[26]

Fundamentally the statement affirms the gracious continuance of the salvation history.[27] When 16:7 is set alongside 7:39; 12:23, 27–28, 31–32; 20:22, it is evident that the "lifting up" of Jesus via his cross to the throne of God brings about the turn of the ages that ushers in the saving sovereignty of God; and so the ancient promises of the sending of the Spirit of the kingdom of God can be fulfilled. We remember, too, the association of the Spirit of God with the saving rule of the Messiah and the Servant of the Lord (Isa. 11:1–10; 42:1–4). The Redeemer Son of God–Son of Man mediates the saving sovereignty of God through the Spirit of Life.

The Paraclete's task in relation to the world is here said to be that of "exposing" it in relation to sin, righteousness, and judgment. Here more clearly than elsewhere we are presented with an elaboration of the concept of a trial of the world before God. The "world" conducted a trial of Jesus, wherein he was declared to be guilty of sedition and blasphemy, and therefore worthy of death (note that the "trial" of Jesus in John was virtually settled in the Sanhedrin meeting, reported in John 11:47–53). Both in the Fourth Gospel and in the synoptics the accounts of the trials of Jesus before the Jews and the Roman governor are written to show that in reality Jesus was the innocent one and that the "world" was condemned by its action. The task of the Paraclete is to "expose" this situation; the trial before the Jews and Pilate accordingly gives place to the tribunal of God in heaven. The elements of this exposure are itemized in John 16:9–11.

"... *of sin, in that they are not believing in me.*" The recognition that the prime sin is unbelief with respect to God's revelation in Christ runs through our Gospel (cf. 1:11; 3:19; 15:22). Such unbelief entails rejection, not ignorance, of the proclamation of Christ. Since the exposure of the world is one of a continuing situation, it has to do not only with the role of the Jewish Sanhedrin and with the decision of Pontius Pilate, but with the attitude of the "world" as such.

"... *of righteousness, inasmuch as I am going away to the Father. ...*" This attestation of righteousness is bound up with the *mode* of Jesus' departure: his lifting up on a cross, which to the world was a demonstration of his unrighteousness, proved to be the means of his exaltation to heaven by the Father. It was therefore God's reversal of the verdict of men and his attestation of the innocence of Jesus. The justification of Jesus is the vindication of his righteousness in life and his entrance upon righteousness in glory with the Father (see 12:23; 13:31–32; 1 Tim. 3:16). This is the heart of the Easter proclamation. Where the world rejects the testimony, their "joy" at being rid of Jesus (John 16:20) is, in Blank's words, "the joy of the damned."[28] Where the testimony is received they experience the joy of the forgiven.

"... *of judgment, inasmuch as the prince of this world has been judged.*" We are clearly directed back to 12:31: the judgment of the world took place when the Son of Man was "lifted up" and the prince of this world was "thrown out." He was rejected as the Son of Man was installed by the Father as Lord and mediator of the saving sovereignty. The Paraclete brings to light that this entails the judgment of the world, inasmuch as its submission to the "prince of this world" led not only to its rejection of the Son of God, but to its becoming the tool for his murder. Its continued failure to acknowledge Jesus as the Lord of the world, installed by God, implicates it in the judgment that took place in the cross and resurrection of Jesus. Like its "prince," its cause is lost; *it has been judged.*

John 16:12–15

I have many things to say to you, but you cannot endure them now; but when he, the Spirit of truth, comes, he will guide you in the entire truth. He will not speak on his own authority, but he will speak all he hears, and he will disclose to you the things that are coming. He will glorify me, inasmuch as he will receive what is from me and disclose it to you. All that the Father has is mine; that is why I said that he will take what is from me and disclose it to you.

The last Paraclete passage forms a climax to the rest, and brings together the teaching concerning the Spirit's ministry for the church.

"The Spirit of truth" will guide the followers of Jesus "in the entire truth," i.e., truth made known by Jesus. The emphasis falls on the word "entire": the truth has been disclosed by Jesus to his disciples, but their grasp of it is limited. The Paraclete will lead them to comprehend the depths and heights of the revelation not yet perceived. This revelation will be not his own, but one that he will "hear." Its source is stated in vv. 14–15: the Paraclete receives from Jesus what he imparts to the disciples, just as Jesus received it from the Father. J. Becker interprets this as a departure from the earlier sayings regarding the Paraclete; he holds that whereas in 14:26 the Paraclete reminds the disciples of a finished revelation from the Lord on earth, here he is to communicate revelation yet to be received from the Risen Lord in heaven.[29] On the contrary, the emphasis throughout the Gospel on the message of Jesus as constituting the revelation of the Father is so consistent and compelling (see e.g., 3:32–35; 7:16–18; 8:26–29; 12:47–50) that it is to be presumed that the same standpoint is maintained here, namely, that the one revelation of God in Christ is the content of that which the Spirit is to convey to the disciples. The significance of 16:13 is its acknowledgement that the Spirit participates in the task of communicating the revelation to the church by virtue of his relation to Jesus, just as Jesus communicated it by virtue of his relation to the Father. Porsch puts it concisely:

Jesus brings the truth, and makes it present through his coming into the world; the Spirit-Paraclete opens up this truth and creates the entrance into it for the believers.[30]

As to the statement, "He will disclose to you the things that are coming," this is best understood not exclusively of the eschatological future, but of "the new order that results from the departure of Jesus."[31] In Bultmann's terse expression: v. 13 states "the essential significance of the Word . . . it illuminates the future."[32] And of course that embraces the near and the distant future, the time of the church to the consummation of the age. *That*, it so happens, is the theme of the book of Revelation.

(9) John 20:22: *The Mission of the Spirit and the Mission of the Church*

> After saying this he breathed in them [*enephysēsen . . . autois*] and said to them, "Receive (the) Holy Spirit."

The context of the passage is to be remembered. The crucified Jesus has risen from the dead. In four economical sentences the evangelist describes the appearance of the Risen Lord to the disciples and how he bestows the peace of the saving sovereignty now established, commissions the disciples for their mission, grants them the Holy Spirit, and gives authority in proclamation of the good news. The Gospel could have ended at that point, and would have ended, but for the desire to tell the story of Thomas and so round off the Gospel with Thomas' confession.

The pertinence of this observation is to indicate that the Gospel reaches its climax in the account of the resurrection of Jesus and the fulfillment of his promise of the coming of the Paraclete. This is what the brief statement, "Receive the Holy Spirit" signifies.

A symbolic sign accompanies the gift of the Spirit: "he breathed in them." The expression is unusual; all agree that it harks back to Genesis 2:7 and Ezekiel 37:9–10. In the former passage God "breathed into the nostrils of Adam the breath of life," so completing the creation of man. In the latter Ezekiel bids the wind (*ruach* = wind = spirit) to "breathe into these slain that they may live," and it happened: "breath came into them, they came to life and rose to their feet, a mighty army." In John's narrative the symbolic action represents the impartation of the Holy Spirit, and with him the life of the new age. New age and new creation are complementary eschatological ideas. Strictly speaking, however, this is not the beginning of the new creation, but rather the beginning of the incorporation of humanity into that new creation which came into being in Christ in his Easter and is actualized in believers by the Holy Spirit (cf. 2 Cor. 5:17).

This action, accordingly, cannot be narrowed in significance, as though it were solely for the disciple group, to enable
them to fulfill their commission and proclamation stated in
John 20:21 and 23.[33] Nor is it to be regarded as a symbolic promise of the gift of the Spirit, later to be fulfilled at Pentecost.[34] Nor
should it be viewed as a *partial* bestowal of the Spirit who is to
be *fully* given at Pentecost.[35] This kind of exegesis entails a
division between Easter and Pentecost that is theologically un-
justifiable and places a wedge between John and Luke. Granted
that Luke's narrative in Acts 2 entails a distance of fifty days
between the resurrection and the outpouring of the Spirit, Luke
himself binds the sending of the Spirit to Easter in Acts 2:33:

> The Jesus we speak of has been raised by God. . . . Exalted thus at
> God's right hand he received the Holy Spirit from the Father and
> poured out this which you see and hear.

The outpouring of the Spirit accordingly is the act of the Risen
Lord! We should not overlook that both John and Luke are capable of accommodating chronology to theology when it seems
right to do so. John's setting the cleansing of the temple in his
programmatic chapter 2 is an example of this. If we did not
possess the book of Acts we should never dream that Luke
placed a period between the resurrection and ascension of
Jesus, for his account of Easter gives no hint of passage of days
and rather gives the impression that all the resurrection appearances and the ascension of Jesus took place on Easter Day
(Luke 24).

My own conclusion is that the Fourth Evangelist, in his narrative of the resurrection in John 20, was above all concerned
to show that the Risen Lord fulfilled his promise of bestowing
the Holy Spirit on his church. It *happened,* fully and decisively,
without any need of amplification at a later date. From this
point of view John's narrative can rightly be described as "the
Johannine Pentecost."[36] For many reasons I see no reason to
doubt the historicity of the Lukan account in Acts 2, especially
in light of its congruence with the significance of Pentecost as
the day of celebrating the giving of the law at Mount Sinai; as
Israel heard the word of the old covenant amidst the flames of
fire (according to tradition in all the languages of the world!),
so the company of the new covenant received the Spirit's power
to proclaim the message of the new covenant in tongues for the

whole world to hear.[37] Both John and Luke were informed theologians, and their accounts of the sending of the Spirit should be judged accordingly.[38]

CONCLUSION

The ministry of the Holy Spirit as portrayed in the Fourth Gospel is complex, but it is comprehensible when the earlier sayings on the Spirit in the Gospel are seen in light of the specifically Johannine teaching on the Spirit-Paraclete in the later discourses.

The Christ who baptizes with the Spirit must first achieve redemption for the world and thereby complete his mission of establishing the saving sovereignty of God. Only then can the Spirit of the kingdom be sent and the mission of Christ be continued in the world through the church.

As the supreme witness to Jesus, the Spirit-Paraclete unveils to the church the heights and depths of the revelation in and through Jesus and thereby enables the church both to grasp it and to testify of it to the world. By the power of the Spirit's ministry, the ongoing trial of Jesus and his church becomes reversed in the trial of the world by the exalted Christ; through the joint testimony of church and Spirit, people become convicted of their sin and of the righteousness of Jesus, and so repent as the guilty before the tribunal of God.

This results in a union by the Spirit with the living Lord, hence the communication to the repentant of the life of the saving sovereignty. In turn that entails union with those reconciled in Christ to the Father. Thereby they are enabled to worship the Father in the Spirit and in the truth of Christ, and to rejoice in the sacramental fellowship of the people of Christ through baptism and the Lord's Supper.

The Easter-Pentecost gift of the Spirit is the end of the beginning of the saving sovereignty of God in Christ. His name "the other Paraclete" has led to viewing him as the "*alter ego*" of Jesus, "the other I." This is legitimate, as long as the temptation is resisted of *identifying* the Risen Lord with the Holy Spirit. It is equally questionable to adopt the common view of regarding him as the *presence* of Jesus in the church. Representations in the Gospel of the abiding of the believer in Jesus as Jesus is in the Father (e.g., 6:57; 17:20–23), and of the dwelling of the Father and the Son in the believer, without confusion of persons (14:23), militate against this. The ancient view that such sayings are to be interpreted of the dwelling of the Father, Son, and Holy Spirit in the church and in the individual is to be pondered. As Augustine stated it:

> The Holy Spirit also makes a dwelling with the Father and the Son; he is at home in every way, like God in his temple. The God of the Trinity, the Father, the Son and the Holy Spirit, comes to us when we come to him.[39]

So the church, commissioned and authorized by the Risen Lord, is renewed by the Holy Spirit to pursue its mission to the world in his holy fellowship. The glory of Christ in his death-resurrection-exaltation is revealed through the church by the ever-present aid of the Holy Spirit, who is the Advocate, the Counselor, the Encourager, the Revealer, the Helper from heaven.

NOTES TO 4

1. See Mark 1:8, 12; 3:29; 12:36; 13:11.

2. Matthew 1:18, 20; 3:11, 16; 4:1; 10:20; 12:18, 28, 31, 32; 22:43; 28:19.

3. Luke 1:15, 35, 41, 67; 2:25, 26, 27; 3:16, 22; 4:1, 14, 18; 10:21; 11:13; 12:10, 12.

4. John 1:32, 33 (twice); 3:5, 6, 8 (twice), 34; 4:23, 24; 6:63 (twice); 7:39 (twice); 14:17, 26; 15:26; 16:7–11, 12–15; 20:22.

5. On this procedure of the evangelist see O. Cullmann, *The Johannine Circle*, London: SCM, 1976, p. 14; J. L. Martyn, *History and Theology in the Fourth Gospel*, 2d ed., Nashville: Abingdon, 1979, p. 129; D. M. Smith, *John*, Proclamation Commentaries, Philadelphia: Fortress, 1976, pp. 55–56.

6. Blank, *Krisis*, p. 310; see further pp. 198–226, 310–16. On this concept of the trial scene in the Gospel of John see especially T. Preiss, "Justification in Johannine Thought," in *Life in Christ*, London: SCM, 1954, pp. 9–31; F. Porsch, *Pneuma und Wort*, Frankfurt: Knecht, 1974, pp. 222–27; I. de la Potterie, *La Vérité dans Saint Jean*, Rome: Biblical Institute Press, 1977, 336–39, 396–99; A. A. Trites, *The New Testament Concept of Witness*, Cambridge: Cambridge University Press, 1977, 78–128; G. M. Burge, *The Anointed Community*, Grand Rapids: Eerdmans, 1987, pp. 36–38.

7. Porsch, *Pneuma und Wort*, p. 224.

8. Ibid.

9. So in Justin Martyr's *Dialogue with Trypho*, 8, 49; see also *m. Sotah* 9.15; *m. Eduyoth* 8.7, 8, 49.

10. Midrash, *Lev. Rab.* 15.2.

11. Burge, *Anointed Community*, p. 84.
12. Ibid., 166–67.
13. Ibid., 168.
14. E. Hoskyns, *The Fourth Gospel*, 2d ed., ed. H. Davey, London: Faber & Faber, 1947, p. 215.
15. Such is the reading of Deut. 27:3 in the Samaritan Pentateuch. In the Masoretic text it is Ebal. The Samaritan tradition could be right, the name may have been changed through anti-Samaritan motives.
16. Dodd, *Interpretation*, p. 314.
17. A. Schlatter, *Der Evangelist Johannes*, 2d ed., Stuttgart: Calwer, 1948, p. 126.
18. Bultmann, *Gospel of John*, pp. 190–92.
19. See H. Windisch, *The Spirit-Paraclete in the Fourth Gospel*, Philadelphia: Fortress, 1968, pp. 1–26.
20. J. Behm, "*pneuma*," *TDNT*, vol. 5, p. 803.
21. Translation by H. C. Kee in *O. T. Pseudepigrapha*, vol. 1, ed. by J. H. Charlesworth, New York: Doubleday, 1983, p. 800.
22. So Porsch, *Pneuma und Wort*, p. 243, following de la Potterie, *Vérité*, p. 130.
23. Bultmann, *Gospel of John*, p. 626.
24. Porsch, *Pneuma und Wort*, p. 270.
25. W. F. Howard, *Christianity According to St. John*, London: Duckworth, 1943, p. 76; also *Interpreter's Bible*, vol. 7, pp. 730–31.
26. Porsch, *Pneuma und Wort*, p. 279. The same interpretation is given by Brown, *According to John*, vol. 2, pp. 710–11, and J. Blank, *Gospel According to St. John*, 2 vols., NTSR 8–9, New York: Crossroad, 1981, vol. 2, p. 135.
27. So E. Bammel, "Jesus und der Paraklet in Joh. 16," in *Christ and the Spirit in the New Testament. Festschrift C. F. D. Moule*, Cambridge: Cambridge University Press, 1973, p. 209.
28. Blank, *Krisis*, p. 338.
29. J. Becker, *Das Evangelium des Johannes*, vol. 2, p. 498.
30. Porsch, *Pneuma und Wort*, p. 300.
31. So Hoskyns, *Fourth Gospel*, p. 487.
32. Bultmann, *Gospel of John*, p. 575.
33. So D. E. Holwerda, *The Holy Spirit and Eschatology in the Gospel of John*, Kampen: Kok, 1959, p. 24.
34. W. Hendriksen, *Exposition of the Gospel According to John*, 2 vols., Grand Rapids: Baker, 1954, vol. 2, p. 461. So G. Ladd, *A Theology of the New Testament*, Grand Rapids: Eerdmans, 1974, p. 289.
35. F. Godet, *Commentary on the Gospel of St. John*, trans. T. Dwight, Edinburgh: T. & T. Clark, 1899–1900, vol. 2, p. 422; B. F. Westcott, *The Gospel According to St. John*, London: Murray, 1881, pp. 350–51; F. F. Bruce, *The Gospel of John*, Basingstoke: Pickering & Inglis, 1983, 2d ed.
36. Bishop Cassien's work, *Le Pentecôte Johannique*, Paris: Editeurs Réunis, 1939, gave the impulse to the use of this expression. See also, in cautious agreement, A. Corell, *Consummatum Est*, London: SPCK, 1958 (and New York: Macmillan, 1959), p. 38; Dodd, *Interpretation*, p. 430, n. 1, modified somewhat in C. H. Dodd, *Historical Tradition in the*

Fourth Gospel, Cambridge: Cambridge University Press, 1953, p. 144, n. 1; Schnackenburg, *Gospel According to St. John,* vol. 3, p. 325.

37. See J. H. E. Hull, *The Holy Spirit in the Acts of the Apostles,* London: Lutterworth, 1967, pp. 48–56.

38. For an excellent review of the varied interpretations of John 20:22, see Burge, *Anointed Community,* pp. 116–46.

39. *In Io.* 76.4.

CHAPTER 5

SACRAMENTS IN THE FOURTH GOSPEL

THE PLACE OF THE SACRAMENTS of baptism and the Lord's Supper in the Fourth Gospel is a hotly contested subject. At least three main views have been maintained regarding this, and many shades of interpretations deviate from the main groups.

(1) First, it has been urged that the Fourth Evangelist is either not interested in the sacraments of the church or hostile to them. Bultmann tersely expressed his own conviction about this: "The sacraments play no role in John."[1] R. Kysar suggested that the evangelist was not so much *anti*-sacramental as *a*-sacramental: he did not know or practice the sacraments.[2] It is pointed out that there is no specific command in the Gospel to baptize, such as the missionary commission of Matthew 28:18–20; no command to celebrate the Lord's Supper; no account of the baptism of Jesus; and in the description of the Last Supper, no mention of the Passover or of the bread and wine and their significance for the death of Jesus. Admittedly the references in John 3:22, 26, and 4:1 to a baptizing ministry of Jesus reflect a baptismal practice in the church, but its importance is diminished by the comment in 4:2 that it was the disciples of Jesus who baptized, not Jesus himself. The one apparently clear reference to baptism on the lips of Jesus, namely, John 3:5, is thought to have been modified by an editor. The evangelist, it is said, simply wrote, "Unless one is born of the Spirit one cannot enter the kingdom of God"; the editor added the two little words, "water and" ("the Spirit"), and so made of it a baptismal utterance.

In a similar manner the discourse on the Bread of Life in chapter 6 is claimed to have been originally without reference to the Lord's Supper till the passage in vv. 51–58 was added, with its statement on the necessity of eating the flesh and drinking the blood of Jesus to gain the life of the divine sovereignty. The lack of mention of the bread and wine and the interpretative sayings of Jesus concerning them in the Last Supper is explained as due to the evangelist's substituting for it the account of the footwashing and/or the prayer of Jesus in chapter 17.[3]

(2) In contrast to the view that the Fourth Evangelist was not interested in the Christian sacraments, there are those who hold that John was *profoundly* interested in them, and that references to the sacraments are scattered through the whole length of the Gospel. The chief protagonist of this interpretation is Oscar Cullmann, who has influenced many by his expositions.[4] He revived certain patristic interpretations of John's Gospel in the endeavor to show that from first to last the evangelist was concerned to relate the narratives of the ministry of Jesus to baptism and the Lord's Supper. This, Cullmann believed, was due to John's desire to demonstrate the connection between the earthly life of Jesus and the church's experience of the Risen Lord. The presence of Christ among his people is actualized in the experience of worship, and early Christian worship was especially characterized by the Lord's Supper and baptism. Cullmann's examination of the Fourth Gospel led him to the conviction that sacramental allusions partake of the warp and woof of the Gospel chiefly through the evangelist's use of symbolism and double meanings. Raymond Brown, while considering that Cullmann's exegesis at times left much to be desired, agreed that a certain sacramental symbolism pervades the Gospel; only in this way could the evangelist impart his sacramental theology and remain faithful to the literary form of a Gospel.

> He could not interpolate sacramental theology into the Gospel story by anachronistic and extraneous additions, but he could show the sacramental undertones of the words and works of Jesus that were already part of the Gospel traditions.[5]

(3) Between the two foregoing positions there is a majority view that the evangelist valued the two sacraments, but as in most other doctrines and elements of the life of the church

which he presented, his chief concern was to demonstrate their relation to Christ. In his Gospel, therefore, he introduced them in an indirect manner, but in such fashion as to highlight their significance for the understanding of Jesus as Redeemer and the believer's total dependence on him for the obtaining of the life to which they bear witness. This interpretation I believe to be correct. The clearest example of this indirect manner of referring to the sacraments occurs in the witness of John the Baptist to Jesus. The fact that John baptized is openly stated, and even discussed (1:25–26). His ministry of baptism is declared to be for the purpose of preparing Israel for the appearance of the hidden Messiah and to make him known (1:26–27). It was precisely in the baptism of Jesus that his identity was revealed to John (1:31): the vision of the descent of the Spirit on Jesus at his baptism showed him to be the one destined to baptize with the Spirit, the Lamb of God, and the Son of God; and to this John bore public witness (1:32–34). The evangelist makes no mention that the scene of the revelation of Jesus as the promised deliverer was actually his baptism at John's hand; nevertheless, every Christian reader of the Gospel would have known that fact, since the ministry of John and his baptism of Jesus were integral elements of the early kerygma (see Acts 10:37–38).

This mode of indirect allusion to baptism in relation to Christ (i.e., as a Christian sacrament) applies to the Lord's Supper in the Gospel. That the discourse of chapter 6 has relation to the Eucharist is acknowledged by all students of the Gospel. So clear is it in the final section of the chapter (vv. 51–58) that a considerable number of scholars have viewed that part as added to an earlier Bread of Life discourse to make the link with the Eucharist explicit. Yet it is easy to overlook the fact that the discourse is primarily an exposition of the "sign" of the feeding of the multitude in the wilderness, and like all other discourses attached to the signs of the Gospel it is a sign of *Jesus and the saving sovereignty of God,* not a sign of the Lord's Supper. When attention is concentrated on the eucharistic elements instead of on Jesus encountered in the Eucharist, the point of the discourse is liable to be seriously misunderstood.

The indirect manner of expounding the Lord's Supper in chapter 6 and the concentration of attention on its christological significance are in harmony with the evangelist's narration of the events of the Last Supper. It is to be remembered that the brief accounts of the Last Supper in the synoptic Gospels are a reflection of their use in worship—and indeed for guidance in celebrations of the Lord's Supper. It is more than likely that the preservation of the Upper Room discourses is due to their frequent use in the context of the Lord's Supper. It is not entirely surprising, then, in view of the evangelist's known selectivity of gospel traditions, that instead of repeating the brief words of the institution known throughout all the churches, he chose to reproduce *teaching that gave their meaning*. It is commonly agreed that this is the most plausible reason for John's recounting at the beginning of the discourses the detailed narrative of the footwashing; he gave this, not to *replace* the eucharistic acts and words of Jesus but rather to *interpret* them in light of the footwashing, and so, in Schnackenburg's words, "to impart a doctrine to the community that celebrated the Eucharist."[6] A similar answer was given by A. Lacomara to the question why no mention is made by John of Jesus' words about the new covenant, which feature so prominently in the synoptic accounts of the Last Supper; in his view John reproduced the *teaching* which gave the significance of the covenant, in a manner comparable to his procedure in the discourse on the Bread of Life in chapter 6:

> As in John 6 we have an extended commentary on the words, "This is my body . . . this is my blood," so in the chapters of the Farewell Discourse we have an extended commentary on the words "of the new covenant."[7]

Sacramental theologians have found in the Fourth Gospel more references to baptism than to the Lord's Supper, doubtless because of the relatively frequent mention of water in the Gospel. This can, however, lead astray, since it disposes the enthusiast to see baptism every time water is mentioned. This may be illustrated by the use made of the two passages, John 4:14 and 7:37–38:

> Everyone who drinks this water will thirst again; but whoever drinks the water that I shall give him will never thirst; the water that I shall give him will become in him a spring of water, welling up to eternal life (4:14).

> If anyone is thirsty, let him come to me; and let the one who believes on me drink. As the scripture said, "Rivers of living water will flow from his heart" (7:37–38).

The former passage is considered by Cullmann to reflect the giving of the Spirit *in baptism*, for John 3:5 teaches that the Spirit is bestowed in baptism, and John 7:37–39 is "certainly to be related to baptism."[8] On the contrary, there is not a hint of baptism in the latter passage. That saying is set in the Festival of Tabernacles, when recollection was vividly made of God's provision of water to drink in the wilderness and the promise of "living water" in abundance in the time of the kingdom of God. Both sayings, in fact, show how the evangelist can refer to the bestowal of life through the Spirit without mention of baptism. Cullmann acknowledges that the feature of water given for *drinking* makes it difficult to apply the two passages to *baptism*, but he adduces the fact that in many Gnostic sects the baptismal water was drunk(!). The observation could be extended: there were others besides Gnostics who regarded baptismal water as good medicine, for in the second century onward it became customary to exorcise the water and bless it, and we hear of Christians drinking it. It is dangerous to assume that wherever water is mentioned in the Gospel, there baptism is in view.

Admittedly it is more plausible to see in the healing of the paralytic beside the pool of Bethesda (John 5:1–9) and the giving of sight to the blind man who washed his eyes in the pool of Siloam (9:1–7) illustrations of the application of baptism to converts. That was general in the older churches of Christendom. Yet it is by no means clear that the evangelist intended to refer to baptism in these healings. The link with the pool of Bethesda was due to the sick man's vain hopes of being healed there; but Jesus neither commanded him to get into the pool nor made any reference to its water, but he healed him simply by his powerful word. In the discourse that follows the healing no hint of baptism is found; rather, this and the healing of the officer's son are treated as signs of the Lord's power to give life to the dead and to exercise judgment as Son of Man and Son of God. The same holds true of the giving of sight to the man born blind. The event is stated to be a sign of Jesus as the light of the world (9:5). That Jesus sent the man to the pool of Siloam to wash off the "clay" he had put on his eyes points not to baptism as the means of enlightenment, but to Jesus as the spiritual Siloam. The name *Siloam* is a Greek equivalent of the Hebrew term *shiloach*, a passive participle meaning "sent," and it related to a discharge of water into the pool. The evangelist saw the fitness in the situation that a blind man gained his sight at a place called "Sent," for the healing took place not through the washing of mud from his eyes, but through the One Sent by God to bring to the world the revelation and the salvation of God. As we saw earlier, the concept of Jesus as the representative sent by God to humankind is the most prominent christological feature in the Fourth Gospel: the Christ has been sent as God's emissary for the world's healing and the receiving of life eternal; that is far more in line with the evangelist's intention in recounting this sign than is directing attention to baptism.

The action of Jesus which comes closest to a symbol of baptism is his washing of the feet of the disciples during the Last Supper in the Upper Room (13:1–20). An ancient tradition has seen allusions to both baptism and the Lord's Supper in the statement, "He who has bathed does not need to wash, except for his feet" (v. 10). Two washings were seen here: the first a bath by which one is made wholly clean, understood as baptism, the other a lesser cleansing needed for sins committed after baptism, which is granted in the Eucharist. We now know, however, that the phrase "except for the feet," in v. 10, is unlikely to have been originally in the text of the Gospel, and is probably due to an early scribe failing to realize that *the washing of the feet by Jesus symbolizes a complete washing gained through a bath.* Any allusion to the Lord's Supper is highly improbable; as J. Michl observed, "A Footwashing would be quite a remarkable symbol for the tasting of the flesh and blood of Jesus."[9] But what of its relation to baptism? Modern scholars who believe that baptism is mirrored in this event tend to qualify the interpretation. Westcott was content to see in the footwashing a "foreshadowing" of Christian baptism.[10] J. A. T. Robinson considered that the action of Jesus represented the universal baptism that Jesus was about to accomplish in his death, which is the ground of the church's baptism and makes it sufficient for salvation.[11] E. Lohmeyer saw in it the eschatological word and deed of Jesus that brings cleansing and the consecration of the disciples for the calling of apostleship.[12] Against all such interpretations it is evident to most exegetes that the point of the narrative is christological rather than sacramental; it points to the redemptive death of Jesus rather than to the rite that is a reflection of it. Schnackenburg, who once advocated the baptismal interpretation of the footwashing, came to abandon it, and wrote:

> His external act has a very deep inner meaning, as Peter begins to sense, but it would be wrong to infer more from Jesus' suggestion than the fact that his giving of himself in death and the saving activity of that death are represented in the "washing." . . . The washing of the disciples' feet is interpreted in the Christological and soteriological sense as a symbolic action in which Jesus makes his offering of himself in death graphic and effective, not in a sacramental manner, but in virtue of his love, which his disciples experience to the extreme limit.[13]

The last of the uncertain passages in the Gospel thought to relate to the sacraments is the soldier's spear thrust into the side of Jesus on the cross, as a result of which blood and water flowed from his side (19:34–35). From the time of Chrysostom onward it has been common to see in the water and the blood from the side of Jesus the true initiation of the sacraments of baptism and the Lord's Supper, and many modern scholars believe that such was the evangelist's intention in narrating this incident. If we are to speak of the evangelist's *primary* intention in the passage, I judge that that is extremely doubtful. The record of the soldiers' restraint in not smashing the legs of Jesus and the thrusting of the lance into his side were recorded to show the fulfillment of Old Testament scriptures; first, those which tell how the Passover lamb should be eaten (Exod. 12:46; Num. 9:12), possibly also God's care for the righteous sufferer (Ps. 34:20, and Zech. 12:10). It was important to the evangelist to show that Jesus died as God's Passover Lamb (cf. 1:29); and it was equally important to report the issue of blood and water from the side of Jesus, for that demonstrated the reality of the death of Jesus and thus the fact that he was a man of flesh and blood—a real man. The closely parallel passage, 1 John 5:6–9, similarly declares the witness of the water and blood of Jesus to the incarnation of the Son of God. G. Richter has urged that in 1 John 5:6, "This is he who came through water and blood . . . not in the water only, but in the water and blood," the writer is describing not two different *events*, namely, the baptism and the death of Jesus, but two *elements* of a single condition, namely, that Jesus came from God as a man having *both water and blood.*[14]

This interpretation is adopted by most scholars, certainly with respect to John 19:34–35, but many still feel that a sacramental reference can be seen on a secondary level. I confess to finding it difficult, even on a secondary level. In the New Testament references to the Eucharist normally include *flesh* and blood, or *body* and blood; and to relate the water from the side of Jesus to baptism seems to be unreal, not least when one bears in mind that in the New Testament baptism is thought of in terms of immersion. If the evangelist really had in view a secondary application of the water and the blood, it is more plausibly related to the gift of eternal life which the Son of God came to make available to humankind. That would be in harmony with the entire Gospel. Such was the conviction of C. H. Dodd. For him the blood and water that issued from Jesus was a "sign" of life that flows from the crucified and Risen Christ.[15] And that is the direction in which Schnackenburg looks:

> The blood is, presumably, a sign of Jesus' saving death (cf. 1 Jn. 1:7), and the water is symbolic of Spirit and life (cf. John 4:14, 7:38), but both are most intimately connected.[16]

That is a cautious, yet deeply significant conclusion to draw in relation to the "sign" of the water and the blood. On that note the Johannine account of the passion of Jesus reaches a fitting end.

We turn to the single clear reference to baptism in the Fourth Gospel, John 3:5, following on the parallel statement of John 3:3:

> Amen, amen I tell you, unless one is begotten from above he cannot see the kingdom of God.

> Amen, amen I tell you, unless one is begotten of water and Spirit he cannot enter the kingdom of God.

It has often been maintained that v. 3 is a Johannine development of Matthew 18:3 or Mark 10:15, or of a comparable saying in the tradition. The moot point is how "comparable" the saying might be. It is necessary to note that the concept of being begotten "from above" (from God) is not a simple translation of becoming like a child, but is an adaptation of *the eschatological hope of a new creation*. The Jews were familiar with the application of this concept to people, as e.g., when they said that God makes people "new creatures" when he heals them of their infirmities.[17] In the use of the concept in the teaching of Jesus, the eschatological element was always present; so e.g., in Matthew 19:28, where the familiar expression "kingdom of God" is replaced by the term *palingenesia,* "regeneration," which is Matthew's equivalent of "new world" or "new age." Paul preserves this understanding when he writes to the Corinthian believers: "Where anyone is united to Christ there is a new world; the old order has gone, and a new order has already begun" (2 Cor. 5:17, NEB). For the Gospel writers the saving sovereignty of God has come into being through the redeeming action of Christ, and those whom God renews experience it now.

In response to the request of Nicodemus for an explanation of the statement in v. 3 Jesus expounds being begotten "from above" as being begotten "of water and Spirit." What is the relation between "water" and "Spirit" here? Origen suggested that in this passage "water" differs from "Spirit" only in "notion" (*epinoia*), not "substance."[18] Calvin similarly interpreted water and Spirit as meaning the same thing, comparable to "Spirit and fire" in the preaching of John the Baptist.[19] Odeberg held that the water stands for the celestial waters, viewed in mystical Judaism as corresponding to the semen of the fleshly being; to be begotten "of water and Spirit" means rebirth of spiritual seed, as in 1 John 3:9.[20] A popular interpretation has it that water represents human birth, whether with respect to the semen of man or waters in the womb, in contrast to birth from the Spirit; this, however, overlooks that the whole expression "of water and Spirit" defines the manner in which one is born "from above." Suggestions like these do not do justice to the text and have not commended themselves to scholarly opinion. It would seem that the text relates birth "from above" to baptism *and* the Holy Spirit. With this Bultmann agreed, but he urged that the reference to water baptism is alien to the context and attributed it to the hand of his "ecclesiastical redactor."[21] More cautiously Bernard viewed the mention of water as due to *the evangelist,*[22] an idea that has been widely taken up of late.[23] The suggestion is interesting but not provable. If the text be taken as it stands, there is much to be said for the interpretation of Bengel, which is frequently echoed in one form or another by British writers: "Water denotes the baptism of John into (i.e., preparing for) Christ Jesus."[24] Such a view assumes

that entry into the kingdom of God is on the basis of baptism
in water, accompanied by repentance, and baptism in the Holy
Spirit. The link between water and Spirit in eschatological hope
is deeply rooted in Jewish thought, as can be seen in Ezekiel
36:25–27 and apocalyptic writings (e.g., Jub. 1:23; Ps. Sol. 18:6;
Test. Judah 24:3), but above all in the literature and practices
of the Qumran community, who sought to unite cleansing and
the gift of the Spirit with immersions and repentance as they
began to "see" the kingdom of God.[25] The need for cleansing
and the expectation of the renewal of the Holy Spirit, accordingly,
was in the air during the period of Jesus and the primitive church.

It is important to observe that baptism features prominently
in John 3. H. Thyen has pointed out that the chapter falls naturally into two sections which have a parallel structure. It really
begins in the closing short paragraph of chapter 2, thus:

A. (1) 2:23–25, a Report which provides the key to the dialogue that follows;
(2) 3:1–12, Dialogue of Jesus with Nicodemus;
(3) 3:13–21, Monologue, giving "the voice of Christ."
B. (1) 3:22–24, a Report on the situations of Jesus and John
the Baptist
(2) 3:25–30, Dialogue of John with his disciples
(3) 3:31–36, Monologue giving "the voice of Christ."[26]

It will be seen from this analysis of the chapter that the evangelist has composed the discourse principally by setting two
dialogues together, each followed by a meditation on the significance of the mission of Jesus to bring salvation to the world.
The dialogues of Jesus with Nicodemus and of John the Baptist
with his disciples are both concerned about the baptisms of
John and of Jesus, though from very different points of view.
This is a pointer as to how the evangelist wishes his readers to
understand the thrust of the conversation of Jesus with Nicodemus: Pharisees like him ought not to stand aloof from the
call to repentance issued by John and by Jesus for entry into the
kingdom of God, for *everybody* is in need of God's forgiveness
and the recreating work of the Holy Spirit.

In *the situation of the ministry of Jesus* these gifts are separate, as the evangelist knows full well (cf. 7:39), but it is a division determined by the tension of the "now and not yet" of the
saving sovereignty. In *the time of the church* for which John is
writing, the gifts are conjoined, since the Lord by his death and

resurrection has achieved a once-for-all cleansing and has sent the Spirit of the Kingdom: the person who is baptized in faith in the Son of Man, exalted via his cross to heaven, becomes a new creature by the Spirit, "sees" the kingdom, and in Christ has life eternal (John 3:14–15).

As in the case of baptism, so with the Lord's Supper, there are passages capable of yielding a connection with the sacrament, but they are even less plausible than the former. The sign of the changing of the water into wine is one such incident. It is noted that reference is made to the fact that the hour of Jesus has not yet come, hence the event points to the death of Christ; that is the hour in which water will be turned into wine and the foundation laid for the Eucharist. Accordingly, the wine of Cana is a pointer to the wine of the Lord's Supper, the blood which Christ shed for the forgiveness of sins.[27] One would have thought that a more obvious motif in the narrative is the quality and abundance of the wine enjoyed by the wedding party, emphasized also in the description of the feast of the kingdom in Isaiah 25:6–9. The provision of the wine instead of water of purification is a sign of the joyous feast of the Kingdom which Jesus inaugurated in his ministry.

The miracle of the wine is associated by the evangelist with the cleansing of the temple, which also constitutes a sign, although it is non-miraculous. If it is asked of what it is a sign, the answer is contained in the statement of Jesus to the Jewish rulers. They demand, "What sign can you show us as authority for doing these things?" He replies, "Destroy this temple, and in three days I will raise it up." The evangelist adds, "He was speaking of the temple of his body" (2:21). From this observation Cullmann rightly draws the conclusion that the worship of the community of Christ's people has its center in the crucified and Risen Christ. He goes on to affirm, however, that *the community* assumes in worship the form of the body of the crucified and Risen Christ, and in view of its connection with the Cana miracle the reference to Christ's body would extend also to *the body of Christ present in the Eucharist.*[28] This is exegesis uncontrolled by care for the distinctiveness of Johannine thought. There is no indication in the Gospel that John thought of the church as the Body of Christ. As Bultmann observed regarding v. 19: "It is not possible that 'body' should refer to the community in the Pauline sense, since the object of 'destroy' and 'raise' must be one and the same."[29] The new temple thus is the Risen Lord himself, not the church. There is no thought of the Eucharist in the passage.

Similar comment has to be made on the suggestion that the words of Jesus in John 4:34, "My food is to do the will of him who sent me and to complete his work," refer to the Lord's Supper. The statement alludes to the disciples' return with food for Jesus to eat; they misunderstood what Jesus said about his food just as the Samaritan woman misunderstood what Jesus said about living water. Jesus lived for the joy of doing his Father's will, i.e., carrying out the mission on which he had been sent. Certainly that is to find its completion in his death and resurrection, but that is no warrant for reading an allusion to the Eucharist in these words.

It is a relief to turn from these speculations to the one passage in the Gospel of John in which Eucharistic reference is unmistakably to be discerned: the discourse on the Bread of Life in John 6. It is scarcely possible, nor is it necessary, for us to embark on the exegesis of the chapter in detail; we are interested primarily in the bearing it has on the Lord's Supper. That comment, however, is not exactly helpful, for the entire chapter, as redacted by the evangelist, is a unity. The two "signs" narrated at its beginning are both related to the discourse that follows. "The theme of John 6 is Christology," wrote H. Thyen.[30] That applies to the feeding miracle, as Léon Dufour remarked: "The miracle is above all the occasion of manifesting the mystery of the person of Jesus."[31] But the same is true of the walking on the sea miracle, with its climactic *Egō eimi*—"I am." And it is the central meaning of the discourse.

The key features of the discourse are as follows:

(a) The bread that Jesus gives is compared with the manna given to Israel in the wilderness. Hecklers listening to Jesus reminded him that their fathers ate "bread from heaven," and asked what *he* can do. They could cite tradition for their question. The Midrash stated:

> As the first Redeemer (i.e., Moses) brought down the manna . . . so will the last Redeemer (i.e., the Messiah).

Jesus reminded them that in fact it was God, not Moses, who gave that bread; he gives now the true bread from heaven, and that bread gives life to the world.

(b) It is with that in mind that we must read v. 35:

I am the bread of Life; he who comes to me will never become hungry, and he who believes in me will never again become thirsty.

Jews were used to thinking of the law as bread which should be eaten, and some at least identified the manna with the Torah. Jesus identified himself with the bread of God, and so speaks of having come down from heaven (like the manna!) to fulfill God's mission, which is to give life to all who believe and to raise them in the last day. It will be observed that the language thus far is in terms of the Lord's gift of life to believers, and no mention is made of the Eucharist.

(c) The Jews took offense at the claim of Jesus to be the bread that came down from heaven. How could this be so, since he was Joseph's son (John 6:41–42)?

The mystery of the incarnation of the Son of God wholly eluded them. Jesus then pressed a further point: the fathers ate the manna in the wilderness—and died; but whoever eats the bread from heaven will not die. "The bread," he says, "which I shall give is my flesh, given for the life of the world" (vv. 50–51). Here for the first time in the discourse it is stated that life will be available to the world on the ground that the one who is the Bread of Life is to give his own life as a sacrifice on behalf of the world. Accordingly, the language changes to relate to this new standpoint: whoever wishes to receive the life which the incarnate Redeemer gives must *eat his flesh* and *drink his blood.* Observe the development of language from v. 35 through v. 51: he who "comes" to Jesus will never become hungry, and he who "believes" will never again become thirsty; in light of the death of Jesus, "coming" and "believing" are replaced by "eating" and "drinking," and the object of faith is the Christ in his sacrificial offering of body and blood for the life of the world.

(d) Eating the flesh of the Lord and drinking his blood result in mutual abiding of the believer and Christ—a concept very close to the Pauline understanding of *koinōnia,* i.e., deepest fellowship with the Lord (cf. Gal. 2:19–20). It is a relationship analogous to that of the Son and the Father: as the Son lives "through" the Father, i.e., has his life from and is sustained by the Father, so the believer has life from and is sustained by the Son (v. 57).

(e) In v. 63 a startling statement is made in light of the offense at the teaching taken by a number of the followers of Jesus:

> It is the Spirit who gives life, the flesh is useless; the words that I
> have spoken to you are Spirit and life.

That must mean that the flesh alone, even of the Son of Man, does not achieve the end which God has purposed, namely, giving life to the world. The incarnation of the Son of God must issue in crucifixion-resurrection-exaltation and the sending of the Holy Spirit for God and humanity to be united in Christ in the kingdom of God. The "words" of Jesus—in the discourse in particular—are "Spirit and life" for those who receive them in faith, since they receive the Spirit and life of which he speaks.

Attempts to isolate vv. 51–58 from the discourse, as though vv. 1–50 were metaphorical but vv. 51–58 were sacramental, are contrary to the manifest intention of the evangelist. In fact the whole chapter can be understood without reference to the Eucharist, and the whole can be interpreted of the Eucharist. The concept of Jesus as the Bread of Life can be related not alone to Jewish thought but to other cultures of the nearer and remoter East. The most remarkable parallel to John 6, however, is found in an utterance of Rabbi Hillel, son of Gamaliel III (not the famous Hillel of earlier times). He astonished his contemporaries by saying, "There shall be no Messiah for Israel, for they have already eaten him in the days of Hezekiah."[32] Whether Hillel intended by this to counteract contemporary Jewish apocalyptic enthusiasts or oppose the Christians is unknown, but it is evident that he denied a future Messiah for Israel on the ground that they had already experienced "messianic" deliverance in the days of King Hezekiah. I was interested to discover that Jewish translations of the Talmud into English substitute the term "enjoyed" for "have eaten": the blessings awaited from the Messiah were *enjoyed* by the Jews in Hezekiah's reign. It is an instructive parallel as to the meaning of "eating" the flesh and drinking the blood of the Son of Man. I am reminded of the statement of Adolf Schlatter in relation to John 6:56:

> What we have to do with his flesh and blood is not chew and swallow, but recognize in his crucified body and poured out blood the ground of our life, that we hang our faith and hope on that body and blood, and draw from there our thinking and willing.[33]

Without doubt this total faith and dependence upon Jesus Christ, the crucified, risen, and exalted Lord, the assurance of forgiveness and his sustaining grace and oneness with us as the Savior and Lover of our souls may be known in life's ordinary ways. But there is equally no doubt that such experience is known and "enjoyed" more intensely, and even uniquely, in the fellowship of Christ's people as they gather about the table of the Lord and share in the bread and the wine.

Those of us who belong to churches which are not accustomed to experience the Lord's Supper as the central feature of worship each Sunday should ponder this fact. In particular, we should reflect on why we feel free to depart from what clearly appears to be an apostolic pattern of worship based on apostolic interpretation of what Jesus meant when he said, "Do this in remembrance of me." As a young theological student I heard a noted Cambridge theologian lecture on the sacraments; in the course of his lecture he stated that since the day of Pentecost there has not been a Sunday in history when the church has not celebrated the Lord's Supper. My immediate reaction was to say to myself, "That's not thanks to the Baptists"—my folk! I have since learned that there has been a long resistance to integrating the Eucharist into Christian worship; neither Archbishop Cranmer, the shaper of the Anglican prayer book, nor Calvin in Geneva could persuade their people to make the celebration of the Lord's Supper integral to Christian worship every Sunday. By contrast, in my own experience, whenever a congregation chooses to adopt a weekly celebration of the Lord's Supper, its members never go back; they "enjoy" the Lord's fellowship in ever fresh ways at his table. If this is the Lord's ordaining, that should be no surprise.

When our people do so meet, let us be sure that from time to time we read and meditate on the discourse of Jesus on the Bread of Life, and the discourses in the Upper Room. They will be an ever new source of inspiration and aid to worship.

NOTES TO 5

1. Bultmann, *Theology of the New Testament*, vol. 2, p. 58.
2. Kysar, *Fourth Evangelist and His Gospel*, p. 259. For related views see the reference in H. Thyen, "Aus de Literatur des Johannesevangeliums," *TR* 44 (1979), p. 103.
3. See especially Bultmann, *Gospel of John*, and *Theology of the New Testament*, vol. 2, pp. 58–59.

4. O. Cullmann, *Early Christian Worship*, trans. A. S. Todd and J. B. Torrance, London: SCM, 1953.

5. Brown, *Gospel According to John*, vol. 1, cxiv.

6. Schnackenburg, *Gospel According to St. John*, vol. 3, p. 46.

7. A. Lacomara, "Deuteronomy and the Farewell Discourse," *CBQ* 36 (1974), p. 84.

8. Cullmann, *Early Christian Worship*, p. 82.

9. J. Michl, "Der Sinn der Fusswaschung," *Bib* 40 (1959), p. 70.

10. Westcott, *Gospel According to St. John*, vol. 1, p. 150.

11. J. A. T. Robinson, "The Significance of the Footwashing," *Neotestamentica et Patristica, Festschrift O. Cullmann*, Leiden: Brill, 1962, pp. 144–45.

12. "Die Fusswaschung," *ZNW* 38 (1939), pp. 83–86.

13. Schnackenburg, *Gospel According to St. John*, vol. 3, pp. 19–20. Such also is the conclusion of G. Richter in his book which reviews the interpretations of the Footwashing through the centuries, *Die Fusswaschung im Johannesevangelium*, Regensburg: Pustet, 1967, especially 195–98. So also in their commentaries, Bultmann, 469–70: Lightfoot, 273; Hoskyns, 436–37; Haenchen, 458; Becker, vol. 2, p. 245; and Blank, vol. 2, p. 24.

14. G. Richter, "Blut und Wasser: Joh 19:34b," p. 125.

15. Dodd, *Interpretation*, p. 428; idem, *Historical Tradition in the Fourth Gospel*, pp. 133–35.

16. Schnackenburg, *Gospel According to St. John*, vol. 3, p. 294.

17. See Strack-Billerbeck, *Das Evangelium nach Matthaus*, Munich: Beck, 1922, pp. 420–23.

18. Origen, *Commentary on John*, vol. 2, pp. 249f. in A. E. Brooke's edition.

19. Calvin, *Commentary on John*, vol. 1, pp. 64–65.

20. H. Odeberg, *The Fourth Gospel Interpreted in Its Relation to Contemporaneous Religious Currents in Palestine and the Hellenistic Oriented World*, Uppsala, 1929, p. 63.

21. Bultmann, *Gospel of John*, p. 139. So also Haenchen, *Das Johannesevangelium*, pp. 218, 227.

22. J. H. Bernard, *Gospel According to St. John*, 2 vols., ICC, Edinburgh: T. & T. Clark, 1928, vol. 1, 104–5.

23. See especially I. de la Potterie, "Naître de l'eau et naître de l'esprit," *Science et Esprit*, 14 (1962) 424–25.

24. J. A. Bengel, *Gnomon of the New Testament*, 5 vols., trans. A. R. Fausset, 1863, vol. 2, p. 175.

25. E.g., 1QS 3:6–9; 1QH 11:12–14. See further G. R. Beasley-Murray, *Baptism in the New Testament*, 2d ed., Grand Rapids: Eerdmans, 1973, pp. 11–18, and for the Qumran community's conviction of experiencing the kingdom of God, H. W. Kuhn, *Enderwartung und Gegenwartiges Heil, Studien zur Umwelt des Neuen Testaments*, vol. 4, Göttingen: Vandenhoeck & Ruprecht, 1966.

26. H. Thyen, "Aus der Literatur zum Johannesevangelium," *TR* 44 (1979), pp. 44–109.

27. So Cullmann, *Early Christian Worship*, pp. 68–69, citing in agreement M. Goguel, *L'Eucharistie des Origines à Justin Martyr*, 1910, p. 196; W. Bauer, *Das Johannesevangelium*, p. 46; C. T. Craig, "Sacramental Interest in the Fourth Gospel," *JBL* (1939), pp. 31ff.

28. Cullmann, *Early Christian Worship*, pp. 73–74.

29. Bultmann, *Gospel of John*, pp. 127–28, n. 6.

30. Thyen, "Aus der Literatur zum Johannesevangelium," pp. 44–109.

31. X. Léon-Dufour, "Le mystère du pain de vie (Jean VI), *RSR* 46 (1958), p. 494.

32. *b. Sanhedrin* 99a.

33. A. Schlatter, *Das Evangelium nach Johannes*, 4th ed., Erläuterungen zum Neuen Testament, vol. 3, Stuttgart: Calwer, 1928, p. 116.

CHAPTER 6

CHURCH AND MINISTRY IN THE FOURTH GOSPEL

THE THEME OF THIS CHAPTER could conceivably cause the raising of eyebrows: Why should space be devoted to the church in view of its comparative absence from the Gospel? "Christology of the Fourth Gospel," "Life Eternal," "Exaltation and Glory of Jesus," "Ministry of the Holy Spirit"—these are subjects of obvious importance for the study of the Fourth Gospel; but where is the church in this Gospel? The word "church" (*ekklēsia*) does not occur in its pages, nor for that matter does the word "apostle" (apart from a solitary instance, where it is used in a purely general sense: "A slave is not greater than his master, nor *one sent* [*apostolos*] greater than he who sent him," 13:16. Further it is frequently pointed out that there is an unusual emphasis in our Gospel on *the individual* and on personal faith for gaining life; in making this emphasis the evangelist has virtually eliminated the expression "kingdom of God," a significant omission in view of the corporate associations of the term. As to the sacraments, the only unambiguous references to baptism in the Gospel relate to the baptism of John the Baptist, to the baptism authorized by Jesus in the early part of his Judaean ministry (3:26; 4:1–2), plus the disputed saying of Jesus (3:5). And despite devoting five chapters to the Last Supper of Jesus with his disciples, John has not left a hint that on that occasion Jesus instituted the Lord's Supper. Bultmann, accordingly, affirmed that in the Gospel of John, "No specifically ecclesiological interest can be detected. There is no interest in cult or organization." In his view such interest as is manifested within the Gospel is expressed in the thought and terminology of Gnosticism.[1]

It is worth comparing this position with scholarly opinion about the church in the synoptic Gospels. It so happens that the term "church" occurs neither in Mark, our earliest Gospel, nor in Luke. It is found twice in Matthew, but one of those does not really count!

The well-known passage in Matthew 18:15–17 gives instruction as to what should be done when two members of the same group quarrel: attempts should be made by the individual concerned to win over the offended "brother," and if they fail, help should be obtained from a third party; if all is in vain it is said, "Tell it to the church." This procedure must originally have related to disciplinary measures to be taken in a local *synagogue*; Jesus did not go about Galilee and Judaea planting churches. The passage was preserved by his followers and later circulated for the guidance of Christian churches in their own procedures. While the application of the saying would not have been limited to professed followers of Jesus among his Jewish hearers, its importance caused it to be preserved for the guidance of Jewish Christians in Palestine, most of whom continued to attend synagogue as well as their own local churches, and for the churches among the nations.[2]

The one clear utterance of Jesus about the church in Matthew is Jesus' declaration to Simon in Matthew 16:18:

> You are Rock,
> and on this rock I will build my church,
> and the gates of Hades will not prevail against it.

That statement, as all know, is one of the most disputed sayings in the Gospels. Further complicating the discussion, many contemporary scholars view it as originally set in a resurrection appearance of Jesus to Peter. I doubt the likelihood of that suggestion, but those who hold it thereby eliminate the use by Jesus of the word "church" from all our Gospel records. It is not surprising, then, that from the time of Adolf von Harnack (at the beginning of this century) the opinion has been maintained by not a few scholars that it is false to attribute the founding of the church to Jesus. For Harnack the issue stands or falls with the authenticity of a few highly dubious New Testament passages, and he had no doubt that they *fell*![3] So arose the slogan,

"Jesus founded no church."[4] But the issue is much more complicated than a few "dubious passages."

Turning to the Fourth Gospel it is true that the word "church" is not to be found within it, but the reality is present in different terms and pictures—more obviously, it so happens, than in the synoptic Gospels. This "reality" is most clearly evident in the allegory of the vine in chapter 15, and it will be instructive briefly to consider it here. The Vine, it will be noted, is Jesus; those who believe in him, and through faith are united with him, are incorporated within the "tree." Further, Jesus is the "true" Vine. Why "true?" In Bultmann's view Jesus is seen as the true Vine over against all other claims to be the Vine of God. Bultmann considered that the background of this imagery is the Gnostic concept of the Vine as the tree of life. In the Mandaean literature it is written: "We are a vine of life, a tree in which there is no lie . . ."; and again, "I am a tender vine . . . and the great Life was my planter."[5] If such notions were in circulation during the time when the Fourth Gospel was written, the assertion that Jesus was the *true* Vine would be particularly significant: in Jesus what was purely mythological has become reality in flesh and blood, and through death and resurrection. The possibility of such a comparison is not to be discounted, but the *origin* of the application of the Vine symbolism to Jesus is not in Hellenistic religion but in the Old Testament, where it frequently appears in relation to Israel (e.g., Hos. 10:1–2; Isa. 5:1–7; Jer. 2:21; Psalm 80). The remarkable feature of these portrayals of Israel as a vine or vineyard planted by God is that in *all* the passages where it is so described the nation is set under the judgment of God for its faithlessness, notably its failure to produce good fruit. The best known example of this is Isaiah's Song of the Vineyard (Isa. 5:1–7). After the description of the care of God in preparing his Vine it is written:

> And now, O inhabitants of Jerusalem and men of Judah,
> Judge between me and my vineyard.
> What more was there to do for my vineyard that I have not
>   done in it?
> Why, when I expected it to produce good grapes, did it
>   produce worthless ones?
> So now let me tell you what I am going to do to my vineyard:
> I will remove its hedge and it will be consumed;
> I will break down its wall and it will become trampled
>   ground (Isa. 5:3–5).

The description of Jesus as the *true* Vine, accordingly, is intended to contrast with Israel's failure to fulfill its calling to be fruitful for God.

There is a brief allusion in the witness of John the Baptist to Jesus as the *Bridegroom* who has come to claim his *Bride* (3:29); that causes joy to John, who was appointed to be the "Friend of the Bridegroom." In the Old Testament Israel is often depicted as the "wife" of God. In John 10:1–18 Jesus is portrayed as the Good Shepherd of the flock, for which he gives his life—again, a transposition of a fundamental concept within the Old Testament of Israel as the flock of God. Without use of imagery the church features in the prayer of Jesus in John 17 as "those who are to believe in me through their word" (v. 20). The Upper Room discourses in John 13–17, while addressed to the Eleven (Judas having departed in 13:30) in their concrete situation immediately prior to the death of Jesus, are spoken to the disciples as representatives of the church that is to be; or, if you will, to the church through the disciples. As Hort put it: "The Twelve sat that evening as representatives of the Ecclesia at large; they were disciples more than they were apostles."[6]

As to the individualism of John, it is an expression of a personal response to the gospel of Christ wholly without tension with respect to the church. The individual believer is incorporated into the church through faith and baptism and the ministry of the Holy Spirit.

It is our task first to consider the contribution of the Fourth Gospel to our understanding of the church.

(1) *The church in John's Gospel is above all understood as rooted in Christ the Redeemer.* It is seen as the fruit of the ministry of Christ in its totality, including his incarnate life and his service to Israel in word and deed, and culminating in his death-resurrection-exaltation for the salvation of the world.

While the gathering of the church from all nations is especially viewed as the outcome of the Lord's redemptive action, the process of gathering takes place from the outset of the ministry of Jesus. (Precisely the same holds true of the inauguration of the saving sovereignty of God through Christ.) Astonishingly enough this process of gathering began in the preincarnate ministry of the Word. In John 1:10–12 we read:

He was in the world,
and the world came into existence through him,

and the world did not know him.
He came to his own domain,
and his own people did not accept him.
But to all who did accept him
he gave authority to become God's children.

This "right to become God's children" employs the symbolism
of adoption into the family of God; people who "received" the
ministry of the Logos formed a company of the Word before the
Word became incarnate. Such "believers," whether from the
people of the old covenant or from those outside it, together
prefigured the church of the Word made flesh. It is implied
that in due time they will surely take their place in the latter's
company.

The work of gathering the renewed people of God com-
menced in the calling of the earliest disciples of Jesus (John
1:35–51). The mention at this point that he gave to Simon the
name "Rock" hints that in the call of these men a first step was
taken in the formation of the church.[7] It is not to be overlooked
that the common term for followers of Jesus in our Gospel is
"disciples," both for the Twelve and for believers not called to
share his ministry in the same way as they were. They learn
even in their early stages of discipleship that they belong to the
flock of Jesus (10:1–5) and that they are able to enter into the
new worship that he was introducing beyond the confines of
Jerusalem's temple and the sacred site on Mount Gerizim
(4:21, 23, 24). Yet the "hour that now is" awaits the hour of
eschatological accomplishment, when the temple of stone is
replaced by the risen Body of the Christ as the place where
God is met and experienced in joyous and redeeming fellowship (2:19). Then it is that the Shepherd who gave his life for
his flock will lead his sheep to green pastures and bestow
upon them the life of God's kingdom of salvation (10:10ff.).
Then it is that he will call "sheep" of other lands to belong to
the one flock of God's grace (10:16). Then, too, disciples will
become branches of the true Vine, and in union with the
Risen Lord they will bear much fruit (15:1–17). That hour of
eschatological accomplishment has become the "now" of
the church, standing as it does between the achievement of
redemption and final salvation in the continuing presence of
its Lord.

(2) *The church is the fellowship of those who receive and keep the word of Christ.*

Self-evidently the hallmark of the church in the Fourth Gospel is faith in the Son of God, who was sent from God to be the Revealer and Redeemer of humankind (John 3:16). Such faith, however, goes beyond a simple profession made in the presence of others; the Gospel emphasizes the necessity of continuing in faith and adhering to the word of Christ. The account of the feeding of the multitude and the discourse on the Bread of Life end in the defection of many "disciples" of Jesus who took offense at his instruction. "This teaching is impossible," they said, "Who can listen to it?" When Jesus asked his close associates if they also wished to join them, Peter replied, "Lord, to whom can we go? You have words of eternal life" (6:68). To receive such words is to belong to the fellowship of him who is the Way, the Truth, and the Life (14:6). And that presumes a continued walking along the Way, remaining in the truth, and living in communion with the Lord.

Exactly that is the message of Jesus to Jewish hearers who, at the Festival of Tabernacles, professed faith in him:

> If you continue in the revelation I have brought, you really are my disciples, and you will come to know the truth, and the truth will set you free (8:31–32).

Such continuance is a settled determination to live in and by (*meinete*, a deliberate action) the word of Christ, followed by a perpetual listening to the word, reflecting on it, holding fast to it, and carrying out its command. The same idea is at the heart of the discourse on the Vine; the believer is to "abide" in Christ, and that includes letting the Lord's words abide in the believer (15:7). Whoever does that "comes to know the truth" and experiences emancipation by the truth. For any instructed in the old covenant that signifies Exodus on the grand scale. As the Exodus under "the first Redeemer" (i.e., Moses) was a release from the slavery of Egypt's land for the freedom of the people of God in the promised land, so the Exodus under "the second Redeemer" (the Messiah) is for the emancipation of the new people of God, drawn from all nations of the earth, for the freedom of the kingdom of God.

Adherence in this manner to the word of Christ inevitably leads to confessing it, and that in a twofold sense of defining the word of truth and declaring it before the world. When Jesus tells Martha that he is the resurrection and the life, he concludes by asking, "Do you believe this?" And Martha says:

> Yes, Master; I have come to believe that you are the Christ, the Son of God, the one who was to come into the world (11:27).

That is just the kind of confessional statement a disciple should make in the church and in the world outside the church. A similar kind of confession is elicited from the blind man to whom Jesus gave sight. After bravely testifying to the reality of the miracle that Jesus had performed on him, he was thrown out of the synagogue by the Pharisees. Jesus sought him and asked him:

> "Do you believe in the Son of Man?" "Who is he, sir?" replied the man. "Tell me, that I may believe in him." Jesus said to him, "You have seen him; it is he who is speaking to you." He said, "I believe, Lord." And he prostrated himself before him (9:35–38).

Thereby a man's pilgrimage of faith was completed; having been born blind, he gained sight: when questioned about it he could only refer to his benefactor as "*the man* called Jesus"; later he said that he was *a prophet* (v. 17), then *one sent from God* (v. 33), and finally *the Son of Man*, whom he addressed as *kyrios* ("Lord," vv. 37–38).

Whoever makes that kind of pilgrimage of faith soon finds that the fellowship of Christ's confessors is divided from the world precisely by the truth that the church confesses. From the prologue onward the contrast between the recipients of the word of truth and the world that rejects it is illustrated again and again. The tension increases as the ministry of Jesus advances, until the representatives of the "world," in the narrative the Jewish leaders, determine that he must die (11:47–53). In the Upper Room discourses the disciples learn that they must be prepared for the same kind of hostility to be directed to them as Jesus himself endured:

> If the world hates you, realize that it has hated me before it hated you . . . (15:18).

> They will put you out of the synagogue; indeed, the hour is coming when anyone who kills you will suppose that he is offering a service to God. And these things they will do because they never knew the Father, nor me (16:2–3).

In the period when the Gospel was composed, that kind of opposition to the church had become an experienced reality. It is reflected in the notorious "Blessing of the Heretics," the Twelfth of the Eighteen Benedictions, which Jews were expected to recite each day and which were included in the worship of synagogue services every sabbath. The prayer became modified to read thus:

> For apostates let there be no hope, and the dominion of arrogance do thou speedily root out in our days; and let the Nazarenes and heretics perish as in a moment; let them be blotted out of the book of the living and let them not be written with the righteous. Blessed art thou, O Lord, who humblest the arrogant.

We are uncertain as to the date when this form of the prayer was authorized; it is commonly thought to have been approved toward the end of the first century. It is also uncertain to what extent and how speedily it affected the relations between the churches and the Jewish synagogues. At all events the mounting opposition of the Jewish leaders to the church led the evangelist to expose the nature and cause of this hostility, to show how the revelation brought by Jesus answers the Jewish objections, and to encourage the churches to maintain their witness to Israel despite the sufferings they endured at Jewish hands.[8]

(3) *The church is the fellowship of those who in Christ have the life of the saving sovereignty of God and the hope of its final fulfillment.*

This affirmation is warranted in light of the eschatological nature of the redemptive ministry of Jesus and his death and resurrection. The emphasis of the Gospel falls on the death-resurrection-exaltation of Jesus for the salvation of humankind, but intimations of its presence in the ministry of Jesus run throughout the Gospel. Dramatic examples of this are seen in utterances of Jesus during the Festival of Tabernacles. The blessings experienced by Israel in the wilderness wanderings and anticipations of their repetition in the end of the age are declared to find present fulfillment in him:

> If anyone is thirsty, let him come to me; and let the one
>   who believes in me drink.
> As the scripture said,
> "Rivers of living water will flow out of his heart" (7:37–38).

And again:

> I am the Light of the world;
> whoever follows me will not walk in the dark
> but will have the Light of life (8:12).

The first saying recalls the water that came from the rock when the Israelites were in desperate need of water in the wilderness and Ezekiel's prophecy of the stream of living water that is to flow from the temple in the kingdom of God (Ezek. 47). The second harks back to the pillar of cloud and fire that was with the Israelites in the wilderness, and the light of God's presence in the Kingdom of the end (Isa. 60:19–20). Both relate to the gift of life: the former specifically to the Holy Spirit as the giver of life (John 7:39), and the latter to the presence of Christ as guide through earthly pilgrimage to the final kingdom of God. Both are addressed to the people as individuals, but both relate to believers as members of God's people who inherit his saving sovereignty.

Individual and corporate examples of the gift of life are seen in the picture of the Shepherd and his flock. As the Door, Jesus gives entrance to the pastures of the flock, which symbolize life in its fullness in the kingdom of God (10:9–10); so also the laying down of the Shepherd's life for the sheep leads to the kind of fellowship with Christ that he, as Son of God, has with the Father (10:14–15). As the crucified Savior, "lifted up" to heaven via his cross, the Son of Man draws all peoples to himself—for fellowship with him in life, and fuller fellowship in his presence in death. Most notable of all is the saying of Jesus in John 14:1–3:

> Stop letting your hearts be in turmoil; keep on believing in God, and keep on believing in me. In my Father's house there are many dwellings: if it were otherwise I would have told you, for I am going to make ready a place for you. And if I go and make a place ready for you I shall come again and take you with me to my home, that you also may be where I am.

This is the simplest representation in the Bible of the Christian hope: the Lord goes to prepare a place for his people in his Father's house, and he is to come again and take them all home. Admittedly, it is a pretty large home, having something of the dimensions of the City of God depicted in the book of Revelation; but it is *home* for the family of God, and there are plenty of rooms for all!

(4) *The church is the fellowship of those who have been loved to the limit and who are called to love in the same kind of way.*

    The obligation of members of the church to love one another as Christ loved them is unique to the Fourth Gospel. In the synoptic Gospels Jesus united two Old Testament commands to make of them one: the so-called Shema, which was the Jewish creed, confessing the Lord to be the one and only God, who is to be loved with heart and soul and might, and Leviticus 19:18, "You must love your neighbor as yourself" (Mark 12:28–31). In the Fourth Gospel the latter command is given a more profound dimension:

> Love one another; as I have loved you, you also must love one another.
> By this everyone will come to know that you are my disciples, if you have love among one another (13:34–35, cf. 15:12–17).

In what sense is the command "new"? The old command was part of the old covenant; this command is the law of the new covenant. As the commands of the Mosaic law were given to Israel as their part in the covenant by which they became God's people, so the "new command" is the obligation of the people of the new covenant in response to the redemption of Christ. It is the *standard* of love, however, which makes the new command distinctive: "*as I have loved you.*" Love of self is a powerful instinct, but it cannot rise to the heights of the divine love for humankind revealed in the cross of Christ; and the noblest self-regarding love cannot compare with the outflow of love from the Redeemer who draws his own to him.

(5) *The church is the fellowship of those united to Christ and therefore to one another.*

Here is another characteristic of the church which is wholly grounded in the person of Christ and his redemptive action on behalf of the world. It is clearly intimated in the picture of Jesus as the "Good Shepherd" who gives his life for the sake of the sheep; this he does, not only for the sheep of Israel's fold, but for those of other sheepfolds, and all are to become *one flock* under *one Shepherd* (10:16). John sees this truth in the callous statement of Caiaphas that it is better for one man to die for the people than the whole nation perish (11:50). John views this statement as an unconscious prophecy: Jesus is to die on behalf of his own people, but not for them alone, but that he should "*gather into one* the scattered children of God" (11:51–52).

It is, however, in the Prayer of Consecration, John 17, that the concern of the Lord for the unity of the church comes to its highest expression. The petition for unity is adumbrated in the prayer relating to the disciples, v. 11:

> Holy Father, keep them in your name, the name that you have given me, that they may be one, just as we are one.

This prayer is expanded in the petition for "those who are to believe in me through their word":

> I make request . . . that they all may be one, just as you, Father, are in me and I am in you, that they also may be in us, that the world may believe that you sent me.
> And the glory which you have given me I have given them, that they may be one, just as we are one, I in them and you in me, that they may be perfected into one, that the world may know that you sent me, and have loved them just as you have loved me (17:20–23).

The unity for which Jesus prayed, "that they all may be one," is defined in the clauses: "just as you, Father, are in me and I am in you, that they also may be in us." It is evident that such a unity is beyond the power of any group or association of human beings to contrive. A unity that is rooted in the being of God can come about only through the miracle-working, re-demptive action of God in Christ. It *has* to be a gift of God, and precisely such a gift is intimated in the text:

> The glory which you have given me I have given them—that they may be one as we are one (17:22).

Whatever the nature of that "glory" of Christ may be, whether his incarnate glory or the eternal life from God which he brought, it is plainly bestowed by the Redeemer-Revealer. In virtue of this bestowal sinful men and women are able to participate in the holy fellowship within the Godhead, in the measure possible to human beings, and so a unity with fellow believers who also share in that same fellowship with God becomes possible. Unity with God and unity with those united to God are complementary. One without the other is inconceivable.

The nature of this fellowship with God is stated in the prayer of Jesus in slightly different ways. In v. 21 the standard and means of unity are expressed thus:

As you are in me, and I in you, that they may be in us.

In v. 23, however, it is said:

I in them and you in me.

In the former case the redeemed become one by participating in the fellowship of the Father and the Son; in the latter case it is through their union with the Son—a concept which is in harmony with the mediatorial role of the Son throughout the Gospel. So it is that men and women become "*perfected* into one," a term frequently used of Jesus' *achieving* his work (4:34; 5:36; 17:4). The unity of the church, accordingly, is the fruit of the accomplished redemption of Jesus the Son.

It scarcely needs to be said that such a gift of grace, by which sinful human beings become one in God and with one another, can attain its divinely willed end only in the consummation of God's purpose. Such is hinted—in the closing sentence of the prayer of Jesus:

I have made known to them your name, and will continue to make it known, that the love with which you have loved me may be in them, and I in them (17:26).

Existing as we do in the time between accomplished redemption and the consummation of God's purpose, we have the task of living in the power of the redemption and in light of the consummation. More concretely, it is an integral part of the calling of the church to manifest in its life the unity which God has created in and through Christ among divided humanity. The tension between the life of the church in Christ and its life in the world has been apparent throughout its history, from its beginning to the present day. This is particularly clear in the ministry and writings of its greatest missionary, the apostle Paul. On the one hand, he rejoiced in the sheer miracle of the breaking down of humanity's deepest barriers through Christ, for in the church there is neither Jew nor Greek, slave nor free, male nor female, all are one Body in Christ (Gal. 3:28); on the other hand, for years he was at the heart of the controversy concerning the terms of admission of Gentiles into the church, a controversy that certainly did not end with the decisions of the Council of Jerusalem (Acts 15:22–29). And so through the centuries the church has been engaged in controversies which

have deeply and permanently divided it, resulting in the griev-
ous divisions of our time. It is one of life's mysteries to me
that relatively so few Christians are concerned about this issue,
above all those in North America, where the church scene is
nothing less than chaotic. Paradoxically, the more "evangeli-
cal" churches are, the less they are concerned about brothers
and sisters in Christ in denominations other than their own—I
say "paradoxically," for it is *Jesus*, in the beloved Gospel of John,
who prayed for the church's unity, and through our disinterest
we obliterate its manifestation to the world.

Thank God, giant steps of progress in Christian relations
have been taken in the twentieth century, both in the ecumenical
movement and at grass roots levels among the churches. But
the divided state of the church remains a continuing stumbling
block to the gospel and a perpetual challenge to Christians in
all confessions. As the church becomes the embodiment of
Christ's redemption, enabling the world to *see* the power of
Christ to transform men and women and to bring about the
kind of community that the world needs, people outside the
church will recognize that God has sent Jesus in love for the
human race, and will thus be encouraged to exercise faith and
enter the fellowship of God in Christ.

(6) *The church is a fellowship created from all nations by the
Redeemer of all nations.*

There has been a certain reluctance on the part of Johannine scholars of late to take this affirmation seriously. A growing
conviction has arisen that the Johannine church (or churches)
must have been an isolated Jewish-Christian group, oppressed
by the hostile policies of the Jewish community of which it
formed a part, and that this determined to no small degree its
presentation of "Jesus against the world." According to Wayne
Meeks the Gospel was written to provide reinforcement for the
community's social identity in its isolation from society; its view
of Jesus as "the Stranger from Heaven," who descends for a
period and returns thither, marks him as an alien from all other
people and is found in contexts where the inability of people of
this world to understand and accept Jesus is in mind.[9] It is not
uncommon for the Johannine church to be described as a "con-
venticle,"[10] a term defined in Webster's dictionary as "an assem-
bly for religious worship; especially a secret or illicit meeting for
worship in forms other than those of the established church."

This idea that the Gospel of John reflects a beleaguered sectarian group, reacting negatively to the society in which it is set, simply does not cohere with our findings thus far. Above all, neither is it in keeping with the consciousness of the church that the mission of Christ is for the world, that Christ died and rose for the world's salvation, and that the church which emerged from his redeeming work is, to adapt Pauline language (legitimately!), "one Body in Christ" (Gal. 3:28), created to reveal to the world the reconciling power of God in Christ through which it may be saved.

(7) *The church is the fellowship to which the mission of Christ to the world is entrusted.*

At this point the consideration of the church flows into that of the ministry. The call of the earliest disciples represented an early action of Jesus to gather a group of followers who would receive the message from God that he brought. These disciples he prepared and trained to lead the nascent church in his mission to the world.

The earliest intimation of this intention of Jesus is contained in the account of his dealings with the Samaritans in 4:35–38:

> You say, don't you, "Four months more and harvest comes?" Look, I tell you, lift up your eyes and gaze on the fields; they are white, ready for harvest.

> Already the reaper is receiving his wages and is gathering a crop for life eternal, so that the sower and the reaper may rejoice together. For in this regard the saying is true, "One is the sower and another the reaper."

> I sent you to reap a crop for which you have not toiled: others have worked away, and you have entered into the results of their work.

This group of sayings may well have been brought together by the evangelist under the common theme of mission. They emphasize that the time of harvest has arrived. Harvest is a common eschatological symbol (e.g., Joel 3:13; Mark 4:1–9, 26–29). In v. 36 it is said that the harvester is already receiving "wages" and gathering produce "for life eternal"; i.e., he is bringing men and women under the saving sovereignty of God that they may experience the life eternal under its rule. The statement, "I sent you to reap a crop for which you have not toiled," indicates a sending of the disciples which John has not reported, but which he recognizes has taken place. They have entered into the labors of others who have proclaimed the word of God to Israel; these "others" may include the prophets of earlier times, more particularly John the Baptist in their own time and Jesus himself, to say nothing of the woman at Sychar, now leading the men of the town to meet and listen to Jesus.

A hint of the association of the disciples with Jesus in his mission is contained in 9:4:

> We must work the works of him who sent me while it is day; night is coming, when no one can work.

Here Jesus links his disciples with himself in his mission in the present; the limitation of time in which to fulfill that mission applies especially to himself, but to them also. Both he and they have an "hour" appointed by the Father, which imparts both an assurance and an urgency to their service of God and humanity.[11]

It is, however, in the later part of the Gospel that the crucial sayings relating to ministry occur. In 13:20 we have a typical expression of the authority of a messenger sent by his superior:

> Amen, amen I tell you, he who receives anyone I send receives me, and he who receives me receives the One who sent me.

The saying presumes the twofold factor that (1) Jesus himself has been sent by the Father, and (2) the disciples have been sent by Jesus. The fundamental law of "one sent is as he who sent him" is strengthened by the declaration that disciples on mission have behind them the authority not only of Jesus, but of God also. The saying is related to that in 15:16, which draws the allegory of the vine to a close:

> You did not choose me, but I chose you, and set you aside that you should go forth and yield fruit and that your fruit should remain, so that the Father should give you whatever you ask in my name.

It is noteworthy that the verb in the clause "I set you aside" is used in v. 13 of Jesus' "setting aside" his life for others; in Numbers 8:10 it is used for the ordination of Levites, in Numbers 27:18 for Moses' setting aside Joshua for his task, in Acts 13:47 for the setting aside of the Servant of the Lord for his mission to the nations, and in 1 Timothy 1:12 of Paul's being set aside for apostolic ministry. Bearing in mind the context of the saying in the discourse on the vine that yields the fruit of faith to God, the affirmation, "I have set you aside *that you should go forth . . .*" suggests that the sending of the disciples on mission is to the fore; assurance is given that prayer in the name of Jesus, as they engage in such mission, will be answered by the Father.

These somewhat ambiguous references to mission give way to clear statement in the Jesus' Prayer of Consecration and the appearances of the Risen Lord to the disciples. In 17:18 we read:

As the Father sent me into the world, I also sent them into the world.

In 20:21 it is recorded:

As the Father has sent me, I also send you.

The representative function of the Son, as he is sent to the world from the Father, is transferred to the disciples as they go forth as *his* representatives on mission to the world. It is entirely possible that the double representation of 13:20 is present in this saying, i.e., disciples on mission have behind them the authority of *Jesus*, and therefore of *the Father* who sent him. Westcott drew attention to the force of the perfect tense in "the Father *has sent* me"; it implies a sending in the past that continues to hold good in the present. The Son is still engaged in mission! Westcott concluded:

The apostles were commissioned to carry on Christ's work, and not to begin a new one.[12]

It is a context of this order that is assumed in the breathtaking statement of John 14:12–14:

Amen, amen I tell you, whoever believes in me will do the works that I do; indeed, he will do greater works than these, because I am going to the Father, and whatever you ask in my name I will do, in order that the Father may be glorified in the Son; if you ask me anything in my name I will do it.

It is important to observe that this passage is a single sentence in which the flow of thought is continuous. Disciples will go forth on their mission and will seek the Lord's aid as they do so. Accordingly they will do the works that Jesus did in his ministry, and yet their works will be even greater, for in response to their prayers *he will act through them,* "that the Father may be glorified in the Son," i.e., through the powerful mission that he continues through the disciples. The "greater works" are *the effects in the lives of the people of the spiritual realities that the words of Jesus signify,* namely, the blessings and powers of the kingdom of God which the death and resurrection of Jesus will set free for the world. The first promise of the sending of the Spirit-Paraclete follows this statement. The promise is fulfilled on Easter evening, when the Risen Lord, after commissioning his disciples to become his associates in mission, bestows upon them the Holy Spirit, through whom his own ministry in the flesh was carried out (20:22).

An integral element in the sending of the disciples on mission is the giving of authority to "forgive" and to "retain" sins of those who hear them:

> Whoever's sins you forgive they stand forgiven them; Whoever's sins you hold back, they remain held back (20:23).

Inevitably we recall the similar saying in Matthew 16:19, with its parallel in Matthew 18:18:

> Whatever you bind on earth will be bound in heaven, and whatever you loose on earth will be loosed in heaven.

The sayings in the two Gospels are clearly independent of each other; they employ different language and are set in different contexts, but their meaning is virtually the same. Adolf Schlatter has convincingly shown that in the Matthaean passage the formula "loose and bind" originally described the activity of a judge in binding a guilty person to or loosing an innocent person from the charges brought against them.[13] In Matthew 16:19 it denotes Peter's authority to declare people forgiven or condemned according to their response to the proclamation of the kingdom of God. In the context of commission to mission, John 20:23 expresses essentially the same thought: disciples proclaim forgiveness of sins on the ground of Christ's redeeming acts and judgment on those who reject the revelation and redemption of the Christ.

Chapter 21 of the Gospel is unique in that it has an emphasis on the situation of the church and its leaders beyond anything contained in the body of the Gospel. In keeping with this, the sign that it narrates has to do with the mission of *the church,* not with *Christ* and his salvation as in the signs recorded and expounded in the rest of the Gospel.[14] The chapter appears to be an epilogue to the story of Jesus narrated in chapters 1–20, whether it was written by the evangelist or by a later editor of the school of John.[15]

The opening account of the disciples' fishing expedition has two separate motifs which should be distinguished: first, that of the extraordinary catch of fish, made possible through the guidance of the Risen Lord; second, that of the meal provided by the Lord for the disciples on the shore (vv. 9, 12, 13), which has the nature of a fellowship meal, or even the Eucharist. The central point of the story as presented by the writer is hinted at in the number of large fish caught by the disciples—one hundred and fifty three—together with the observation that the net was not broken, despite the size of the catch. We owe to the learned Jerome the observation:

> Writers on the nature and properties of animals, who have learned "fishing" in either Latin or Greek (one of whom is the most learned poet Oppianus Cilix) say that there are one hundred and fifty-three species of fish.[16]

The claim has been disputed (Oppianus did not make the statement; it was a case of counting the species of fish that he named in his book, and at times that was ambiguous);[17] but it would appear that such an idea was current in early times, and in that case the success of the church's mission to the world could have been adumbrated in the miracle.

Jerome's friend, Augustine, made a different suggestion: the number 153 is the sum of the numbers 1 through 17, which is a triangular number (representing the numbers 1 to 17 by dots on separate lines, and increasing the lines one at a time, they form a triangle). 17 = 10 + 7; in Augustine's view the former represents the 10 commandments, the latter the sevenfold Spirit of God (Isa. 11:2); hence 153 is a numerical symbol for perfection, and so for the perfection of the church.[18]

I forebear to describe further the growing literature on the number 153, but it is plausible that the great haul of fish prefigures the church's mission to the nations. The meal of Jesus with the disciples links the fellowship meals he held in the ministry with those in the resurrection and the church's celebrations of the Lord's Supper, all of which, like the feeding of the multitude in the wilderness, prefigure the feast of the kingdom of God for the nations, described in Isaiah 25:6–9.

The conversation of Jesus with Peter in 21:15–17 is likely to have been private. The disciples disappear from view. It is not impossible, in view of the nature of the conversation, that we have here a description of the appearance of the Lord to Peter referred to by Paul as the first of his appearances to the disciples (1 Cor. 15:3–5). If that be so, it will have taken place on Easter Day (cf. Luke 24:34). The single issue which the Lord has to clarify is Peter's relation to him after the devastatingly emphatic denials of Peter that he had had anything to do with Jesus. There is no need to distinguish between the differing terms for love (*agapaō* and *phileō*) that Jesus and Peter use in their exchange of questions and answers. Suffice it to say that the Lord sifted him to the depths, till all the old self-confidence and assertiveness of Peter drained away. In the end Peter could say no more than that the Lord, who reads the hearts of all, knows that he really does love him. Accordingly the Lord accepted the truth of his protestations of love, and renewed his commission to service in the kingdom and the church.

What, however, are we to make of the terms of the commission given by the Risen Christ to Peter?

Take care of my lambs.
Look after my sheep.
Take care of my sheep.

The traditional understanding of these words by the Roman Catholic Church remains firm to this day. Cornelius a Lapide expressed it with all clarity:

On his departure into heaven Christ here designates his Vicar upon earth and creates Peter the supreme Pontiff, in order that the church may be governed by one Pastor.[19]

The effect of such a statement on Protestants generally is to leave them dumbfounded! The key issue is the meaning of the term "pastor" or "shepherd." J. F. X. Sheehan has urged that its interpretation in this passage is characteristically applied to Israel's rulers. A typical example is 2 Samuel 5:2, where the elders of Israel say to David:

The Lord told you, "You shall *shepherd* my people Israel, and you shall *be prince* over them."

On this basis, according to Sheehan, Peter is appointed by Jesus to rule over the church.[20] One would have thought, however, that the meaning of "shepherd," both as a noun and as a verb, should be interpreted in light of its use in the New Testament, specifically by Jesus and Peter and other apostles. The "model shepherd" is the Good Shepherd, who cares for his sheep and lays down his life for them (John 10:11–14). In 1 Peter 5:2 Peter, as a fellow elder, appeals to the elders of the churches: "Shepherd the flock of God that is among you," virtually citing the Lord's words to him in the resurrection. Paul in similar vein tells the elders of the Ephesian church:

> Keep watch over yourselves and over all the flock, of which the Holy Spirit has made you guardians, to shepherd the church of the Lord (Acts 20:28).

These passages speak in a closely similar manner to the Lord's words to Peter when he restored him to fellowship and ministry. There is no formal difference of meaning in the language by which the Risen Lord confirmed Peter in his calling to be a shepherd of his sheep and that by which Peter and Paul exhorted the pastor-elders to fulfill their calling as shepherds of the flock of God. There is no, therefore, ground for viewing the Lord's commission to Peter in John 21:15–17 as conveying an exclusive authority over the church and its shepherds. The emphasis in this passage is on the restoration of Peter to seek and to care for the sheep of God's flock. In view of Peter's catastrophic experience of fall and subsequent restoration to fellowship with his Lord, he was peculiarly fitted to fulfill the pastoral office to which he was appointed.

That this understanding of Peter's commission is in harmony with the evangelist's intention is indicated by his setting it in immediate juxtaposition with the prophecy as to the way in which Peter would glorify God by his death, for this, too, was probably an independent piece of tradition. Peter is told that at some time in the future he will stretch out his arms—to embrace and be tied to the beam of what will be a cross; he will be led away to be crucified. As God was glorified through the death of Jesus (12:27–28; 13:31–32), so he will be glorified by the death of Peter. Another "good shepherd" will lay down his life for the sheep.

The epilogue closes in the dispelling of a current misunderstanding about the destiny of the Beloved Disciple. When Peter
asked the Lord what was to become of his friend, the Lord's
reply was brusque: "If I should will that he remain until I come,
what is that to you? You follow me" (21:22). On the basis of this
statement, the report had spread among the churches that the
Beloved Disciple was not going to die. The evangelist, however,
points out that Jesus said no such thing; he simply stated, "*If I
should will that he remain* . . . what business is that of yours?"
If that disciple had in fact died, perhaps since the composition
of the Gospel as a whole, the concern of many Christians would
have been comprehensible, hence the evangelist was anxious
to show that that concern was without foundation.

But there's more to the story than that. Peter had been curi-
ous about his friend's future; Jesus had dismissed his curiosity,
with the added command: "*You* follow me." So the last glimpse
we have of the Lord and his disciples is of Jesus walking ahead,
with Peter following, and after him the Beloved Disciple. No
other disciples are mentioned. But the early readers of the Gospel will have known the sequel. Both men became notable witnesses to Christ and his gospel. They followed Jesus, but in
what different ways! Peter, the powerful preacher of the gospel,
the pioneer of the church—through his witness Peter opened
the kingdom of heaven for multitudes, and he completed his
witness to Christ in a martyr's death ("martyr" = "witness"). The
Beloved Disciple, also a faithful witness to Christ and a builder
of the church—but he followed his Lord in quieter ways without
the world taking note; yet his witness to Christ was completed
in the Gospel that most fully reveals the Son of God— "the
Gospel of the Beloved by the Beloved," as one has described it.[21]
In this respect the epilogue gives an ideal picture of the ministry
for ministers of all times: the Lord has a path for every one of his
servants. Their task is not to look at other servants of Christ,
whether in envy or satisfaction that they are not doing as well as
others, but they are to keep their eyes on Jesus (cf. Heb. 12:2,
"looking away off to Jesus"), and they are thus to follow him with
unswerving obedience in the path he has assigned them.[22]

NOTES TO 6

1. Bultmann, *Theology of the New Testament*, vol. 2, p. 91.

2. The commentary of Strack-Billerbeck on Matthew cites much interesting material from rabbinic literature, comparing disciplinary procedures in contemporary Judaism with those laid down in Matt. 18:15–17; see *Das Evangelium nach Matthäus erläutert aus Talmud und Midrasch*, 787–92.

3. *The Constitution and Law of the Church*, tr. F. L. Pogson, London: Williams & Norgate, New York: Putnam, 1910, pp. 3–5.

4. So W. Michaelis, *Täufer, Jesus, Urgemeinde*, 1928, p. 105; Linton, *Das Problem der Urkirche*, 1932, p. 179, cited by R. Newton Flew, whose book, *Jesus and His Church*, London: Epworth, 1943, was directed to this issue; he approached it from an indirect point of view, considering first the implications of the teaching of Jesus and the course of the ministry of Jesus to his death, in which it is not difficult to see the concept of the church coming to the fore with increasing clarity, and so he advanced to the examination of Matt. 16:16–19, and showed its harmony with the word and work of Jesus.

5. *Ginza* 59:39–60:2, and 301:11–14.

6. F. J. A. Hort, *The Christian Ecclesia*, New York: Macmillan, 1898, pp. 30–31.

7. *The Gospel According to St. John*, vol. 1, p. 313.

8. On this issue see the comprehensive article by W. Horbury, "The Benediction of the Minim and Early Jewish-Christian Controversy," *JTS* 33 (1982), pp. 19–61.

9. W. Meeks, "The Man from Heaven in Johannine Sectarianism," *JBL* 91 (1972), pp. 68–69.

10. So e.g., Kysar, *Fourth Evangelist and His Gospel*, pp. 246–48; Brown, *Gospel According to John*, cv–cxi (in part); Käsemann, *Testament of Jesus*.

11. Compare the dictum of Rabbi Tarphon in The Sayings of the Fathers, 2:15: "The day is short, and there is much work to be done, the workers are lazy, and the reward is great, and the Master of the house is urgent."

12. Westcott, *Gospel According to St. John*, vol. 2, pp. 349–50.

13. A. Schlatter, *Der Evangelist Matthäus*, Stuttgart: Calwer, 1948, p. 511.

14. See A. Shaw, "The Breakfast by the Shore and the Mary Magdalene Encounter as Eucharistic Narratives," *JTS* 25 (1974) p. 12: and for the whole episode R. Pesch, *Der reiche Fischfang*, Düsseldorf: Patmos, 1969.

15. For a review of the critical questions relating to John 21 see the articles of H. Thyen, "Aus der Literatur zum Johannesevangelium," *TR* 42 (1977), pp. 213–61, and idem, "Entwicklungen innerhalb johanneischen Theologie und Kirche im Spiegel von Joh 21 und der Lieblingsjünger Texte des Evangeliums," L'évangile de Jean, ed. M. de Jonge, 259–99.

16. Jerome, *Comm on Ezechiel xiv*, Migne, PL 25, 474c.

17. R. M. Grant, "One Hundred Fifty-Three Large Fish," *HTR* 42 (1949), p. 273.

18. *Tract. in Jo.* 122.

19. Cited by E. Hoskyns, *The Fourth Gospel,* p. 557.

20. J. F. X. Sheehan, "Feed my Lambs," *Scripture* 16 (1964), pp. 22–23.

21. Cited by H. Thyen, "Aus der Literatur zum Johannesevangelium," *TR* 42 (1977), pp. 260–61.

22. This is sounder than the suggestion that the evangelist is comparing favorably the Beloved Disciple at the expense of Peter, who is more greatly honored in other churches. There is no hint in chapter 21 that the evangelist wishes to denigrate Peter. The humiliation of Peter in the conversation with Jesus is narrated to show that the unhappy past was all forgiven, and that the Lord had completely reinstated him in his service. Moreover, when this Gospel was published, Peter's shame had been wiped out through his many years of faithful ministry, which reached its climax in his martyr death. That privilege had not been accorded to the Beloved Disciple. Churches had good reason to honor *both* disciples, and to seek to emulate them in their own discipleship and service of Christ.

SCRIPTURE INDEX

JEREMIAH
2:21 104
17:13 68

EZEKIEL
34 42
36:25–27 94
39:9–10 79
47 110
47:1–11 68

DANIEL
7 29

HOSEA
10:1–2 104

JOEL
2:28–32 60
3:13 115

ZECHARIAH
12:10 38, 91
14:8 68

MALACHI
3:1ff. 64
3:1–6 64
4:1 64
4:1–2 64

NEW TESTAMENT

MATTHEW
1:18 82
1:20 82
3:7–12 37
3:11 64, 82
3:16 82
4:1 82
10:19–20 71
10:20 82
10:37 45
10:39 5
10:40 16, 25
12:18 82
12:28 82
12:31 82
12:32 82
15:24 16
16:16–19 123
16:18 103

16:19 118
18:3 92
18:15–17 103, 123
18:18 118
19:28 93
22:43 82
28:18–20 85
28:19 82

MARK
1:8 8
1:12 82
1:15 8
3:29 82
4:1–9 115
8:31 48
8:35 5
8:38 28
9:43 2
9:43–48 2
10 3
10:15 92
10:17–31 3
12:6 16
12:28–31 111
12:36 82
13:9–11 75
13:11 71, 82
13:26 28
14:24 45
14:34–41 47
14:41 46
14:62 28
15:24 49

LUKE
1–2 59
1:15 82
1:35 82
1:41 82
1:67 82
2:25 82
2:26 82
2:27 82
3:16 64, 82
3:22 82
4:1 82
4:14 82
4:18 82
4:26–29 115
9:24 5
10:18 52
10:21 82
11:13 82

DATE DUE			
AUG 24 '92			
NOV 02 '92			
NOV 30 '92			
NOV 30 '92			
MAR 06 '95			
JUN 10			
JUL 06			
DEC 01			
MAY 19			